A RAFT FROM THE OTHER SHORE

NAMU AMIDA BUTSU
"Homage to Amida Buddha"

This is the *nembutsu*, the single phrase that Pure Land followers recite to call upon Amida Buddha's guidance for Birth in the Pure Land. This particular calligraphy was made by Honen himself on the opening page of his greatest work, the *Senchaku Hongan Nembutsu-shu (Passages on the Selection of the Nembutsu in the Original Vow).* Courtesy Rozan-ji Temple, Kyoto. National Treasure of Japan.

A RAFT FROM THE OTHER SHORE

Honen and the Way of Pure Land Buddhism

SHO-ON HATTORI

Revised and Edited by
JONATHAN WATTS & YOSHIHARU TOMATSU

JODO SHU PRESS
Tokyo

Copyright © 2000 by Jodo Shu Press
http://www.jodo.or.jp/j-press/
4-7-4 Shibakoen, Minato-ku,
Tokyo 105-0011
Japan

ISBN 4-88363-329-2 C0015

CONTENTS

PREFACE

Buddhism began when Gautama Siddhartha awakened to the truth of the universe and became Shakyamuni Buddha in the sixth century B.C. in India. He taught the way of truth and liberation to the people of ancient India for forty-five years, passing away at the age of eighty. About a hundred years after he died, the Buddhist community was in a state of schism concerning the *vinaya*, the disciplinary rules for monks, and finally divided into two groups: the conservative and the progressive. Around the first century A.D., two major schools appeared respectively called the Theravada and the Mahayana.

The Theravada school sought to maintain the traditional teachings and practices laid down by the Buddha and was transmitted to Sri Lanka, Bangladesh, Burma, Cambodia, Laos and Thailand; while the Mahayana school sought to interpret the spirit and meaning of the Buddha's enlightenment and was brought to Tibet, China, Vietnam, Korea and Japan. As Buddhism is tolerant by nature, it has spread to various countries, being absorbed by their cultures and creating new types of Buddhism.

Although Japanese Buddhism may not appear to be Buddhism in its Indian sense, it is a true form of Buddhism. It is true because the original Buddhism Shakyamuni Buddha taught was absorbed by Japanese culture and transformed into a unique Japanese form of Buddhism. For example, Indian and Chinese Pure Land schools emphasize meditation practices more strongly than Japanese schools of Pure Land tradition. This is because in India, the *dhyana* tradition of meditation, and in China, Taoistic mysticism, greatly influenced Buddhist teaching. In Japan, when Honen founded the Pure Land school, he emphasized the simple recitation of Amida Buddh's name, and Honen's disciple, Shinran, taught the way of simple faith. Simplicity is one of the characteristics of Japanese culture.

Buddhism was introduced to Japan in the sixth century, but in the early stage of its evolution it was more like Chinese Buddhism. It was during the twelfth to thirteenth century that Buddhism became Japanized. Honen was the first master to promote the creation of genuine Japanese Buddhism. Following him, Shinran founded the True Pure Land school; Dogen organized Zen Buddhism; and Nichiren established the Nichiren denomination. These masters revealed uniquely Japanese types of Buddhism. In this regard, Honen is an important figure in the history of Japanese Buddhism.

This book is a collection of the author's essays contributed to journals and newspapers. The author appreciates the permission to reprint them which has been given by Tokai-gakuen Women's College, Tohokai, Doho University, and the headquarters of the Jodo Shu denomination. Sincere gratitude should be expressed to Jodo Shu Press, which undertook the publication, and to Mrs. Christine Ogawa, who read over the original manuscript and improved its clarity and accuracy of expression.

Sho-on Hattori

PREFACE
to the Second Edition

In the twenty-first century, the dream of dwelling in space may come true, but our home is still the earth, a blue planet in the universe. The fact that we live on one planet suggests that we must live together harmoniously without discrimination based on race or creed. Thanks to the advancement of communications technology, the world has been getting smaller and smaller. Yet the distance in people's mental and spiritual realms seems to be getting wider and wider. Wars and conflicts between nations still persist. Domestic troubles break the peaceful life among members of a family. Individuality might be accepted and respected, but self-assertion, if emphasized too much, brings about unease and confusion in personal life and in society as well. Whilst living in this new age, we are now requested to meditate upon ourselves and our existence once again.

In twelfth century Japan, a Buddhist master named Honen seriously contemplated his existence and awakened to the great compassion of Amida Buddha, thereby gaining ultimate salvation. He made every effort to show the path by which all can liberate themselves to attain peace in their hearts.

This book attempts to present an introduction to Honen's teachings and to Buddhism in general. It was originally published under the title *Honen Shonin and Buddhism* in 1992. The title has now been changed to *A Raft from the Other Shore: Honen and the Way of Pure Land Buddhism*. The author would like to express profound gratitude to Jonathan Watts and Rev. Yoshiharu Tomatsu for reading the manuscript and making significant recommendations for editing as well as Rev. Ryusho Saito for his technical assistance. Without their cooperation and assistance, this new edition would not have come to fore.

Sho-on Hattori
December, 2000

Chapter One

THE LIFE OF HONEN SHONIN

Beginnings

Honen was born in the village of Inaoka in the township of Kume in Mimasaka province, present day Okayama Prefecture, located about four hundred miles west of Kyoto. At his birthplace now stands Tanjo-ji temple.

His father Uruma no Tokikuni was from one of the leading families in the province. He was a local official in charge of police activity to maintain public peace and order. Honen's mother was a daughter of the Hada family, whose ancestors had come from China and whose business was silk products. The Hada family was wealthy and, therefore, one of the powerful families in the province.

Tokikuni and his wife were unable to have children for a long time. In their despair, they sincerely prayed to

Buddha for a child. One night Tokikuni's wife had a strange dream in which she swallowed a razor blade. Tokikuni rejoiced, because he felt it was a good omen predicting the birth of a son.

On April 7, 1133, his wife gave birth to a boy. In the huge Muku tree that stood at the west corner of Tokikuni's house, two white banners appeared out of nowhere and became caught in its branches. A few purple clouds dotted a blue sky. All these seemed to be signs of blessing on Tokikuni's family.

The son was named Seishi-maru, and he was a brave and intelligent boy. The name "Seishi" comes from the Bodhisattva Mahasthamaprapta (Daiseishi-bosatsu), one of the attendants of Amida Buddha, who symbolizes wisdom.

In 1141, when Seishi-maru was nine years old, his father was fatally wounded by Akashi no Sada-akira. Sada-akira was a local official sent by the lord of the province, the Emperor Horikawa, to govern the area. At the moment of death, Tokikuni said to his son, "Don't hate the enemy but become a monk and pray for me and for your deliverance." This tragedy opened up a channel of religious awareness for Seishi-maru.

Seishi-maru was sent to his uncle's temple to carry out the final words of his father. His uncle, Kangaku, was a younger brother of his mother and was the head priest of Bodai-ji temple located about sixty-five miles north of Seishi-maru's birthplace. It was there that Seishi-maru began to study the Buddha's teachings. While teaching Buddhism to him, Kangaku realized that Seishi-maru had great ability and potential to learn more, so he decided to send him to Mt. Hiei, the center of Buddhist study in those days.

Within the Buddhist Establishment

In 1145, at the age of thirteen, Seishi-maru was sent to Mt. Hiei. First, he studied with Jiho-bo Genko in the north valley of the western section of the mountain. Then two years later he became a disciple of Koen at Kudoku-in temple. Seishi-maru was ordained by Koen and studied the Tendai (T'ien-t'ai) Buddhism of Mt. Hiei under him. But Seishi-maru was not satisfied with this, and in 1150, at the age of eighteen, he left Koen and went to study with Jigem-bo Eiku in the Kurodani valley of the same area. There Seishi-maru was named Honen-bo Genku by Eiku and began earnestly to search for the way of religious salvation.

Honen's main concern was not to achieve high social status as was that of many priests in those days. According to biographies of Honen, however, he did attain a high reputation as a monk of great learning on Mt. Hiei. But this was not what he was seeking. What he wanted was to find the way of universal salvation, the way through which everyone together can attain final liberation in the Pure Land.

In 1156, at the age of twenty-four, Honen went to Nara, the ancient capital of Japan, to learn more about Buddhism and to find this way of universal salvation. In route, he visited the Shaka-do hall at Seiryo-ji temple in Saga, a western suburb of Kyoto, to pray for success in finding this way. At the Shaka-do Hall was enshrined a statue of Shakyamuni Buddha. This statue had been brought there from China by Chonen of Todai-ji temple in Nara in 987 and was worshipped by everyone as a sacred image. In Nara, he visited the great temples such as Kofuku-ji and Todai-ji, as well as the great scholar-priests such as Kanga of the Sanron school (San-lun), Zoshun of the Hosso school (Fa-hsiang), and Keiga of the Kegon school (Hua-yen).

Breaking Away

Honen described his life of seeking for "the way" as follows: "Essentially Buddhism includes observation of precepts (*sila*), realization of concentration (*samadhi*), and attainment of wisdom (*prajna*). But I cannot accomplish these three-fold requirements. Is there any other way by which even I could be liberated? I visited many temples and priests, but no one gave me a satisfactory answer. So once again I have come back to the library at Kurodani to study harder than ever to find the way of salvation."

He read all of the Buddhist scriptures (*Tripitaka*) three times and Shan-tao's *Commentary on the Meditation Sutra* five times. It was Shan-tao's text which finally revealed to him the way of universal salvation. This way is the practice of nembutsu. This realization occurred when he was forty-three years old.

The nembutsu had been practiced before Honen at Mt. Hiei and in Nara, but it had only secondary meaning as a religious discipline. No one regarded the nembutsu as an independent practice. They considered it to be one of many disciplines. It was Honen that established the nembutsu as an absolutely independent practice.

After realizing the truth of the nembutsu, Honen left Mt. Hiei for Kyoto and began to spread the teaching of the nembutsu there. In the spring of 1175, he founded Jodo Shu, or the Pure Land Denomination, in Japan. The center of his teaching was at Yoshimizu, where Chion-in, the Head Temple of Jodo Shu, now stands.

A Path for All

Honen's teaching attracted many people. Those who came to Honen's center to listen to his teachings included not only priests and nobles, but also warriors, an ex-robber, fishermen and even prostitutes.

Among the priests attracted to Honen's teaching, Shoku, Shoko, and Shinran are important, because they later developed denominations of Pure Land Buddhism in Japan. Shoku (1177-1247) became Honen's disciple in 1190 at the age of fourteen when Honen was fifty-eight.

He studied Pure Land Buddhism under the guidance of Honen for twenty-three years and is respected as the founder of the Seizan branch of Jodo Shu. Shoko (1162-1238) came to study with Honen in 1197 when he was thirty-six years of age. After learning and succeeding to Honen's teaching, he went to Kyushu and spread the dharma of the nembutsu. He is considered the second patriarch of Jodo Shu, Honen being the first. Shinran (1173-1262) became a disciple of Honen in 1201 at the age of twenty-nine. He is regarded as the founder of Jodoshin-shu, or the True Pure Land Denomination.

The Japanese imperial family's association with Honen occurred when Honen was requested to conduct the ceremony of taking the Buddhist precepts by three emperors: Goshirakawa, Takakura and Gotoba. Among the nobility who were drawn to Honen's teaching, Kujo Kanezane was a well-known and important figure. He held various positions in the aristocratic government of the Heian period and became prime minister in 1189. Kanezane had a chance to participate in the ceremony of taking the precepts from Honen about five times. He was also instrumental in getting the place of Honen's exile changed from Tosa to Sanuki province. Further, it was Kanezane who requested Honen to write a book about the nembutsu, which became the *Senchaku Hongan Nembutsu-shu (Passages on the Selection of the Nembutsu in the Original Vow)*, the basic text of Honen's nembutsu thought.

Kumagai Naozane illustrates the type of warrior influenced by Honen. He was a brave warrior and had killed many people. His great fear was of going to hell after death. However, when he heard Honen's sermon that even a sinful man could attain salvation through the teaching of the nembutsu, he was moved to tears and became Honen's disciple. Masako, wife of warrior Minamoto no Yoritomo, who founded the Kamakura government, was also a follower of Honen.

Among Honen's lay followers, there was a fortune teller named Awanosuke. He was said to be a stupid but faithful devotee of the nembutsu and is considered to be the inventor of the double-stranded *juzu* (rosary), instead of the usual single-stranded *juzu*, which is popular among Jodo Shu followers. One day Honen asked Shoko, "Which nembutsu practice is better Awanosuke's or Honen's?" Shoko replied, "Of course, Honen's nembutsu practice is better than Awanosuke's." Upon hearing this, Honen reproved him, saying, "How long have you been studying the meaning of the nembutsu? There is not the slightest difference between the two, because both of us have the same intention of wanting to attain Birth in the Buddha's Pure Land." This story indicates that the value of the nembutsu lies beyond the grasp of intellectual ability.

Exile

As the teaching of the nembutsu spread throughout the country, old temples such as Enryaku-ji on Mt. Hiei and Kofuku-ji in Nara tried to stop the nembutsu. In the winter of 1204, the priests of Mt. Hiei met together in front of the Main Hall and appealed to the Zasu (chief abbot), Shinsho, to abolish the nembutsu. Honen responded to this by making a document called the *Shichikajo Kishomon (Seven Article Pledge)*. The main points mentioned in this document were not to speak ill of other sects, their teachings and followers; not to behave improperly; and not to teach wrong teachings that the masters (Shakyamuni and Honen) had not presented. The document was signed by 190 disciples to confirm their pledge. As a result of this document, the attack from Mt. Hiei temporarily calmed down.

Kofuku-ji, however, was not satisfied. Gedatsu-bo Jokei of Kasagi wrote the *Kofuku-ji Petition* that included nine errors of the Pure Land Buddhism of Honen. In October of 1205, the priests of Kofuku-ji in Nara sent the document to the Imperial court and appealed for the teaching of the nembutsu to be stopped and for Honen and his disciples to be punished. An Imperial Order was subsequently made stating that there were followers of Honen who misunderstood the master's teaching and who behaved improperly. They should be punished, but as this was their own fault of going against Honen's teaching,

Honen should not be punished.

The priests of Kofuku-ji were not pleased with this. They again appealed in order to persecute Honen's disciples who were understood to have strong attachments to the nembutsu alone and to abuse other sects. A principle disciple of Honen's, Kosai, was actually thrown out of Honen's center, because he taught that one recitation of the nembutsu was sufficient to achieve salvation *(ichinengi)*. His student Gyoku was also thrown out, because he propagated the conduct of breaking the Buddhist precepts and did not respect the vows of other buddhas. Attacks from Kofuku-ji were frequent after this.

The strongest attack against Honen was made on February 18, 1207, when Honen was 75 years old. This stemmed from an incident in the twelfth month of 1206, when the ex-Emperor Gotoba made a pilgrimage to the Kumano shrines. During his absence, two of his ladies in waiting, without his knowledge, attended a nembutsu service conducted by Honen's disciples Juren and Anraku and were moved to become nuns. As a result of Gotoba's ensuing rage, Juren and Anraku were sentenced to death and Honen was exiled to Tosa on the island of Shikoku.

Honen did not hesitate to accept his exile. He actually appreciated it, saying, "My exile is the expression of Imperial courtesy, because otherwise I could not bring the teaching of the nembutsu to the people who have never had the opportunity to meet me and listen to me directly." One of his disciples, Sai-Amidabutsu, told Honen not to practice the nembutsu for a while in order to prevent the old temples from attacking. However, Honen replied, "I will practice the nembutsu even if they put me to death."

Honen left Kyoto on March 16, 1207 for Shikoku. On the way, he taught the nembutsu to the people in such places as Kyo island, Takasago bay in Harima, Muro harbor and Shiaku island. His listeners included fishermen, prostitutes, warriors and villagers. At last, Honen arrived in Sanuki province on Shikoku his place of exile. At first, Honen had been sentenced to exile in Tosa province, but later ex-premier Kanezane was able to change the place to Sanuki because of its milder weather.

Final Journey

On December 8, 1207, an Imperial Order was issued by which Honen was released from his exile on Shikoku island. Still not permitted to return to Kyoto, he stayed at Kachio-dera temple near Osaka for a few months. It was on November 20, 1211 that Honen was finally permitted to enter Kyoto. On January 23, 1212, he wrote the *One Sheet Document (Ichimai-Kishomon)* at the request of Genchi, his closest disciple. In the document, Honen stated the essence of his faith, telling followers that the nembutsu is the ultimate way of universal salvation, so make every effort to practice it without bothering with your own finite knowledge. He passed away two days later on January 25, 1212 at the age of eighty.

Chapter Two

THE WAY OF HONEN SHONIN

A Crisis of Faith

The days during which Honen lived were a transitional
time from the Heian period (794-1192) to the Kamakura
period (1192-1333). This time was also characterized as
the Age of the Final Dharma *(mappo)*. The idea of *mappo*
originated from the Buddhist prediction that as time
passed after Shakyamuni Buddha's death, the teachings of
the Buddha would decline and society would deteriorate.
This passage of time is divided into three periods. The
first is called the Age of Right Dharma *(shobo)*, in which
Buddhist disciplines are strictly observed and the followers are perfectly faithful. The second period is the Age of
Semblance Dharma *(zobo)*, in which the teachings and
disciplines are sincerely carried out but enlightenment is

not attainable. The third period is *mappo*, in which
humanity becomes morally corrupt and religiously degen-
erate.

The essential idea of *mappo* is not simply to divide the
period after the death of the Buddha, but to reflect on the
thought that the more remote we live from the time of
Shakyamuni Buddha, the more difficult it is to accomplish
the required discipline of the Holy One. This indicates
that, although the dharma, or the teaching of the Buddha,
exists as it was originally, it is hard to fulfill because of
changes in social conditions and in human beings themselves. *Mappo* is also understood to be a disorderly and
impure state in which people are incessantly attacked by
feelings of fear and worthlessness. For this reason, *mappo*
is often viewed as the end of the world, a time in which
people see the disappearance of the sacred teachings of
the Buddha that have acted to preserve peace in the world.

The idea of the age of *mappo* seems to have already
taken root in early ninth-century Japan. At first, it prevailed among Buddhist scholars and masters. As time
elapsed, however, it gradually came to be regarded as a
real fact in human history. By the end of the Heian period,
in the twelfth century, the idea had spread throughout the
country.

If we study the political scene during Honen's life, we
realize that there were frequent changes in government
leaders, and bloody revolts often occurred. When the
power struggles among the ruling classes reached a cli-

max, the bloody insurrections of Hogen in 1156 and of Heiji in 1159 were ignited, in which kinsmen of the imperial family, nobles, and warriors fought among each other. After 1159, instead of the Fujiwara family, who had been the ruling power in the country, the warrior classes mainly of the Minamoto and Taira clans came into control. After defeating Minamoto no Yoshitomo (1123-1160), Taira no Kiyomori (1118-1181), chieftain of the Taira clan, became chancellor *(dajodaijin)* in 1167 and boastfully claimed, "One is not a man if he does not belong to the Taira." However, a little more than a decade later in 1185, the Taira clan was vanquished by a Minamoto clansman, Yoshitsune (1159-1189). Thus, the ruling power was brought into the hands of the Minamoto clan. Minamoto no Yoritomo (1147-1199) came into power and became *seii-tai-shogun* (generalissimo) in 1192, establishing a military government at Kamakura and thus beginning the Kamakura period. He was succeeded by his son, Yoriie, who was assassinated in 1203. Then Sanetomo, Yoriie's younger brother, was bestowed the title of *shogun*. However, actual political power was held by the Hojo family.

Such serious, bloody fighting and frequent changes in the ruling classes resulted not only in the loss of power to control and preserve the peace throughout the country but also created a chaotic condition in the society as a whole. As a result, the people of that time vividly envisioned the literal existence of *mappo*.

In addition to the political conflicts, another factor contributed to the feeling of *mappo*. This was the movement of groups of armed monks *(sohei)*. Until the end of the Heian period, large Buddhist monasteries, such as Todai-ji, Kofuku-ji, Enryaku-ji, Miidera (or Onjo-ji) and some of the leading shrines such as the Gion, the Kumano, the Kitano and the Hiyoshi, maintained large standing armies. In their early stages, the *sohei* were used chiefly in disputes between monasteries, but later they began to descend upon the capital, forcing their own interests upon the Court. By the time of Honen, the *sohei* had already been recognized as a nuisance in society.

The activity of the *sohei* indicates that the major monasteries in that day had become secularized and deeply involved in power struggle. They were engaged in destroying, burning, and fighting in their protest against the government, thus bringing about a disorderly state in the entire country.

Besides the political instability and the movement of the *sohei* there was another crucial factor, natural disaster. In 1132, the name of the year was changed to Chojo (Long Gift) in expectation of more favorable circumstances. However, tornadoes and floods continued to cause much damage and many people died of tuberculosis. In 1134, famine attacked the whole country. The imperial court had to distribute rice to the poor. By 1136, famine still continued, and babies were frequently forsaken. In 1143, smallpox spread all over the country. In 1150, strong winds and floods again brought damage. In 1153, there were no crops. In 1155, another famine. In the years 1161, 1163, 1175 and 1177, smallpox epidemics repeatedly ravaged the nation. In 1177, there was a disastrous fire in Kyoto. In 1180, a tornado hit Kyoto. In 1181, another great famine hit from the sixth month of the year. Then a terrible drought lasted until autumn when a great storm hit, and a disastrous failure of crops again caused the people to suffer. In 1185, in the seventh month of the year, a devastating earthquake occurred. The imperial palace and many Buddhist temples in Kyoto were destroyed. These are only a few examples of the natural calamities that happened during Honen's life. They drove the people into a dreadful state of unrest in which they anticipated the coming of *mappo*.

In this way, the teaching of *mappo* became not just a theory but a reality. Political insecurity, the wild conduct of the *sohei*, earthquakes, plagues, famine, floods, looting, murder and arson, all these misfortunes caused the people to believe in the Buddhist prediction of *mappo* stated in the sutras. As such, their main concern was how they could be liberated from such a wretched state. Honen's teaching provided the answer.

A Teaching for the Times

Buddhism is generally understood in two ways. One is that it is the teachings of the Buddha. The other is that it is the way of becoming a buddha, an "enlightened one."

The former concept of Buddhism has its counterpart in other religions, such as Christianity. Buddhism is the teaching that has been revealed by the Buddha Shakyamuni, a historical person, as Christianity is the gospel brought by Jesus Christ, also a historical figure. Even though modern scientific studies show that not every Buddhist scripture prevailing nowadays is genuine, Buddhists hold that these scriptures still contain the truth of the Buddha's enlightenment.

The second definition of Buddhism, the way of becoming an enlightened one, is a unique concept of Buddhism in comparison with Christianity. Christianity is the teaching of God through Jesus Christ but not of the way to become God. Since God is the creator and supreme being in the world, man cannot become God. Christians may assert that God lives within them through faith, but this does not mean that God and man can become identical. However, in Buddhism anyone can become a buddha if s/he awakens to truth. We have buddha-nature (Skt. *buddhata*, Jp. *bussho*) within ourselves, and when we realize it, we can become a buddha. Buddhism is the way for everyone to reveal the buddha-nature within themselves. By following the path of Buddhism, everyone can attain perfect peace or bliss as Shakyamuni Buddha did some two and a half thousand years ago.

After reconsidering the nature of Buddhism, however, Honen reached the point that the teaching should be viewed through its practical value rather than through its theoretical value. However excellent the teaching may be, it is of no use if it cannot be practiced by everyone to attain enlightenment. The final goal of Buddhism is for all to attain enlightenment. Therefore, it cannot be "pure" Buddhism unless it can be carried out by all. Even if the teaching is true doctrinally or logically, it is not true Buddhism if it cannot be followed by everyone to achieve the final goal of Buddhism. After Honen re-examined the doctrines of various denominations, he concluded that their teachings might be true from a doctrinal aspect but were not true when apprehended from the practical point of view, because they were too hard for everyone to fulfill. One of the major problems Honen encountered while seeking the truth of Buddhism was how everyone (man and woman, young and old, poor and rich, able bodied and disabled) could be liberated (or attain enlightenment). From this practical point of view, various denominations in his day did not reveal the true nature of Buddhism. Honen believed that if a teaching were true, it should be the way for everyone to be liberated into the Buddha's state. When the teaching is only for the rich to attain enlightenment, it is not true Buddhism. When it is only for the able, it is not authentic either.

As we have observed, according to Honen, there are at least two steps by which it is possible to grasp the meaning of Buddhism. The first step is that any teaching may be called Buddhism when it is dependent on Buddhist

scriptures. The second step is that even among so-called
Buddhist teachings, the only teaching that may be called
true Buddhism is that which reveals the way of total liberation. It is on this second step that Honen's teaching mainly depends. From Honen's emphasis on universal salvation, the perspectives on Buddhism have become widened
and deepened.

Honen's Pure Land Buddhism may sometimes have
been misleading. It has been said that his teaching is
"Amidaism", not the genuine Buddhism of Shakyamuni.
The Pure Land school puts stress on Amida Buddha and
his power of salvation. People should totally rely on
Amida's grace rather than on their own power. This
approach has been considered by some to be against
Shakyamuni's original teaching, because in his final words
Shakyamuni told his disciples, "Do not rely on others but
rely on yourself." In order to become enlightened and to
attain profound peace, we should follow the precepts and
train ourselves. We should not rely on others. This may be
true in the early stage of Buddhism. However, when we re-
examine and reconsider the "spirit" of Shakyamuni's
teaching, we will come to the point where we realize that
his major concern was the way for everyone to gain
enlightenment or perfect bliss. This spirit of the Buddha
can be expressed as the way of universal salvation. That is,
Buddha's teaching should be the way for everyone to be
liberated into the perfect bliss of buddhahood. From this
perspective, Honen's teaching is not pseudo-Buddhism but

genuine Buddhism

Many Buddhas, One Body

Shakyamuni Buddha

When I was in the United States about three decades ago, a Japanese-American woman came to me and said, "I have heard that the Buddha is considered a man. If that is so, why should we worship the Buddha, a man? In the Christian religion, God is worshipped because He is the only one divine being in the world and He is more than man. I can't understand, therefore, why the Buddhists worship the Buddha who was a man."

Many people, including students and scholars who first come in contact with Buddhism, generally understand the Buddha only through Shakyamuni Buddha who lived in India around the 5th century B.C. He was a man who became enlightened to the truth of the world and so became a buddha. He was born as a prince in the Shakya kingdom of northern India (present day Nepal). He spent his youth in seeking pleasure and leading a luxurious life in the palace. One day when he was twenty-nine years old, upon going out of the castle with his servant, he happened to come across four unexpected incidents. He saw a crippled old man, a sick man, a funeral procession, and some monks. These things upset him and caused him to re-evaluate human life. He realized that the life he had led in the palace, surrounded by beautiful maidens and luxuries, was not the true world but simply a false and illusory state. He chose to become a monk as a result of these incidents, and so began to practice the religious disciplines that prevailed in those days.

For six years he followed various religious practices but could not attain final peace. Reduced to only skin and bone, he almost died. Until one day, he came to a river, bathed himself and then received an offering of milk from a young girl. With renewed strength, he went to sit under a *bodhi* tree (a pippal tree) and started to meditate. Seven weeks later when the morning star shone in the eastern sky, he "awakened" to truth and thus became a buddha. In those days, the term "buddha" was usually used for any-one who became enlightened, rather than to indicate a par-ticular person, like Shakyamuni Buddha.

Starting with an examination of himself and the world in which he lived, he realized he did not live alone but rather he lived by the grace of immeasurable blessings from heaven and earth. He felt the breath and life of the trees, the air and the whole universe surrounding him. He discovered himself to be a part of the great life of the world. Thus he was liberated from the world of bondage and selfish individuality and from the illusory world of unreal shadows. When aware of this truth about ourselves and living in gratitude to others, we come to live in peace. In this sense Shakyamuni stated that every being in the world has buddha-nature by which to attain perfect peace.

After enlightenment, Shakyamuni Buddha began his

mission, wandering about the northern part of India. He
brought the teaching to all people until he passed away at
the age of eighty. This man, Shakyamuni, the lord of the
Shakya clan, is usually considered the Buddha in the original sense. We know his life in human history so we call
him the historical Buddha. When the Buddha is understood in this light, he is respected as a pioneer who
opened a new sphere in human spirituality, as a teacher
who showed us the way to final liberation, and as the ideal
person.

The concept of "buddha", however, is not restricted to
this. Through this historical Buddha, we come to see the
more important figure that reveals itself in the ultimate
nature of the Buddha. In Buddhology, the historical
Shakyamuni Buddha is called the *nirmana-kaya*, or manifested body of Buddha. He is believed to be the person
who appeared on the earth to reveal truth.

Threefold Body of Buddha

When Shakyamuni Buddha, the historical Buddha, died,
his followers discussed whether the Buddha had really disappeared from the earth or not. They contemplated this
crucial problem and concluded that the Buddha himself
did not disappear from the earth at all. He is here on the
earth. Shakyamuni's body might have disappeared from
the earth but he is still alive in his teachings or in the truth
to which he awakened. Thus the Buddha came to be
apprehended in the teachings or Buddhist truth. We cannot

see Shakyamuni Buddha any more, but we can still "see"
him in the truth he left. We call this concept of buddha the
dharma-kaya, or truth body of Buddha.

Now Buddha is also conceived of from another angle.
In order to become a buddha, we have to accomplish two
ideals. One is self-enlightenment, the other is enlightenment of others. This is based on bodhisattva ideals. A
bodhisattva is one who aspires to attain enlightenment. In
order to attain it, s/he should make at least two vows: the
vow to attain enlightenment and the vow to liberate others
or to lead others to the state of enlightenment. When s/he
fulfills these vows, s/he will become a buddha. This is the
Buddha that will be realized as the result of the bodhisattva's austere meritorious practices. This is called the *sambhoga-kaya*, or reward body of Buddha. One of the main
buddhas of this kind is Amida Buddha, who is worshipped
by Pure Land Buddhists.

Thus Buddha can be comprehended from three different angles: the Buddha as a historical person *(nirmana-
kaya)*, as truth itself *(dharma-kaya)*, and as a recompensed
body *(sambhoga-kaya)*. These may be understood as three
aspects of one buddhahood, or the three-bodies (Skt.
trikaya, Jp. *sanjin*) system in Buddhology. The teaching of
the system may vary according to the sutras and denominations, but the concept mentioned above is the basic one.

Each body has its own characteristics. The *nirmana-
kaya* may satisfy scientific minds or sense experience
because of its historical existence, but it may not satisfy

religious minds that seek the "eternal." The *dharma-kaya* may satisfy philosophical or intellectual minds for apprehending transcendental truth, the truth beyond the limitations of time and space. Yet it may not satisfy religious minds that seek the warm heart or compassion of a divine being. In this way, the *sambhoga-kaya* may embody the ideals of both the *nirmana-kaya* and *dharma-kaya*. This Buddha has two excellent qualities, one as eternal truth and one as personal savior. He embodies the personal warmth of the *nirmana-kaya* and the transcendental truth of the *dharma-kaya*.

Thus Buddha may be expressed in different figures but these do not indicate different buddhas. As mentioned above, these are different aspects of one buddha-nature. We may understand the Buddha as Shakyamuni Buddha, the historical figure, but this is only one aspect of Buddha. We should know the true meaning behind Shakyamuni.

Amida Buddha

The Buddha that Honen focuses on mainly is Amida Buddha. Amida Buddha is considered to be a *sambhoga-kaya*, the buddha-body realized after accomplishing the sacred vows of a bodhisattva. According to the *Sutra of Immeasurable Life* (Skt. Larger *Sukhavativyuha Sutra*, Jp. *Muryoju-kyo*), one of the main scriptures of Pure Land Buddhism, Amida Buddha was previously the Bodhisattva Dharmakara (Hozo-bosatsu). At first, he was a king, but upon hearing a sermon by the Buddha Lokeshvararaja

(Sejizaio-nyorai), he resigned his kingship and became a monk. He then established forty-eight vows to become a buddha. After long, austere religious practices, he fulfilled the vows and became the Buddha called Amida. This accomplishment leads to a kind of *sambhoga-kaya*, or reward body of Buddha.

For Honen, however, Amida is not simply a *sambhoga-kaya*. He is the totality of the three-bodies of Buddha *(trikaya)* by nature. Honen believes that all the virtues of the *trikaya* are integrated into one buddha, Amida. Amida is the best manifestation of the truth of buddha-nature. Amida is found in the Sanskrit texts as *amitabha* (infinite light) and *amitayus* (infinite life). This means Amida Buddha is beyond the limitations of time and space. Yet he is both eternal and personal. His liberating power is all over the world. It does not discriminate against anyone. His grace, light and life are everywhere and in every person. He is the great liberator of the world.

Pure Land Buddhists worship Amida, not Shakyamuni, as the central divinity of their faith. They are sometimes criticized for this. They are sometimes called not genuine Buddhists but pseudo-Buddhists. However, this is not true. Pure Land Buddhists are genuine Buddhists. According to Honen, Shakyamuni is important because it is he who reveals the truth of Amida Buddha to us human beings. Basing himself on the *Meditation Sutra* (Skt. *Amitayur-dhyana Sutra*, Jp. *Kammuryoju-kyo*), one

of the main sutras of Pure Land Buddhism, Honen said
that in response to the desires of various individuals,
Shakyamuni gave them contemplative and non-contempla-
tive practices, but in order to save all people, especially in
the later ages after his nirvana, he eventually rejected
them. The one practice which Shakyamuni first gave and
never rejected was the nembutsu. For Honen, not only is
the nembutsu the practice included in Amida Buddha's
Original Vow, it also is the practice that Shakyamuni
entrusted to his disciple Ananda to transmit far into the
future. Therefore, without Shakyamuni's enlightenment,
we could not meet Amida Buddha and could not find the
way of our own liberation. In this way, Honen warns us
not to ignore Shakyamuni but to pay deep respect to him.

Shakyamuni advocated various ways to enlightenment,
and Honen emphasizes that Amida Buddha is the best
because he established the way by which everyone can
attain Birth the "Land of Buddha". This truth is revealed
through the teaching of the nembutsu.

Selecting a Path

Honen's nembutsu is called the *senchaku hongan nembutsu*, "the Nembutsu Selected in the Original Vow". It represents the unique characteristic of his religious thought.
This name indicates three different kinds of nembutsu: (1)
nembutsu, (2) *hongan nembutsu*, and (3) *senchaku hongan
nembutsu*.

First, *nembutsu* includes the various types of nembutsu advocated by many masters and scholars since the beginning of Buddhist history. The term *nembutsu* consists of two characters *nen* and *butsu*. The term *nen* means "concentrating," "recollecting", "aspiring," and "reciting". The term *butsu* indicates the object of *nen* and refers to various buddhas, such as Shakyamuni, the Medicine Buddha (Skt. Tathagata Bhaisajyaguru, Jp. Yakushi-nyorai), Amida and so on. *Butsu* also sometimes includes a buddha's virtues and name. Thus *nembutsu* may mean "to concentrate on a buddha or his virtues", "to recollect the buddha himself", or "to recite the buddha's name".

Hongan nembutsu indicates the nembutsu of Shan-tao (613-681). Shan-tao (Zendo) was a predecessor of and is considered to be the spiritual master of Honen, because Honen was enlightened to the truth of Buddhism by Shan-tao's *Commentary on the Meditation Sutra*. Therefore, it is sometimes asserted that Honen's view and Shan-tao's view of the nembutsu are the same. However, we need to recognize the difference between the two.

Honen's nembutsu is not simply *hongan nembutsu*, but *senchaku hongan nembutsu*, the third type of nembutsu. That is, Honen's nembutsu is different from Shan-tao's in terms of *senchaku*, which literally means "selecting." The literal meaning of the *senchaku hongan nembutsu* is the nembutsu of the Original Vow *(hongan)* that was selected by Amida Buddha. This *senchaku* contains an important concept for us. Through the spirit of *senchaku*, Honen established the nembutsu as the simple invocation of the formula *Namu Amida Butsu*. For Honen this was the ultimate way of salvation.

Let us examine some of the characteristics of Honen's nembutsu.

Simplicity

During the Heian period (794-1185), there were other types of recitation of the name besides *Namu Amida Butsu*, such as *Namu Butsu* (Homage to the Buddha), *Namu Daihi Amida Butsu* (Homage to Amida Buddha of Great Mercy), *Namu Sanjin Sokuichi Amida Nyorai* (Homage to Amida Buddha, Totality of the Three Buddha-bodies) and so on. As recitations of the name, they do not differ from Honen's nembutsu. However, when we observe them through Honen's spirit of *senchaku*, we can understand that he wanted to select the only one that contained all the others.

The other recitations had not been practiced widely and had not held much religious significance in the history of Buddhism. Furthermore, one of the characteristics of Pure Land faith during the Heian period was that various other practices were required in addition to the nembutsu. Honen considered these various other practices superfluous and did not accept them. He required only the formula *Namu Amida Butsu*. Another more important reason why he wanted to establish only this formula is that it was based on the Original Vow *(hongan)* of Amida Buddha.

For this reason, Honen presented the discipline in which the devotee simply recited the formula with faith in the Original Vow in order to attain salvation. Honen thus clearly stated that the nembutsu was the recitation of the holy name of Amida.

Another important meaning of the simple recitation of the name should be understood in relation to the Principle Nembutsu *(rikan)* and the Meditative Nembutsu *(kambutsu)*. During the Heian period, the value of the nembutsu in most cases was found in either the Principle or Meditative Nembutsu. The Recitative Nembutsu was not considered to have any superior significance. Both the Principle and the Meditative Nembutsu required a concentrated mind. This was done in order to meditate upon the supreme form of Amida and the beauties of the Pure Land (Meditative Nembutsu) or to apprehend the ultimate reality of the universe (Principle Nembutsu). In contrast, Honen remarked simply in a letter to Amanoshiro, a lay follower, "The nembutsu does not hold any complicated understanding. We should know nothing but the teaching that we are able to attain Birth in the Pure Land by recitation of the nembutsu." He also informs us in another document, "The nembutsu does not mean to bear in mind the *dharmakaya*, nor to meditate on the supreme form of the Buddha. Rather, it means to 'recite' the name of Amida Buddha with all one's heart. This is called the nembutsu."

Quality

One of the characteristics of the nembutsu of the Heian period was to practice it sixty thousand or one hundred thousand times a day. Its value seems to have been measured by the number of times the devotee practiced it. In contrast, the nembutsu advocated by Honen contained infinite value even in one single recitation. He states in the *Senchaku-shu (Passages on the Selection of the Nembutsu in the Original Vow)* that one nembutsu is "unsurpassed" *(mujo)*. Even though Honen regarded the value of each nembutsu as infinite, he did not deny the practice of recitation of many nembutsu. Indeed, he encouraged the devotee to engage in reciting the nembutsu continuously. To carry out continuous recitation might be construed to mean that Honen emphasized the act *(gyo)* itself. So far as it is understood in this manner, it would have the same tendency as the Heian nembutsu, which stressed the act by which the devotee attained the final state of *samadhi*. Honen, however, did not assert this meaning of the nembutsu. He emphasized the meaning of the recitation in relation to faith and consequently established the significance of one single nembutsu.

Independent and Inclusive

Honen's religious awareness in apprehending the meaning of the nembutsu was deepened and purified by the spiral activities of two opposite kinds of consciousness: selection and integration. First, let us look at his nembutsu in the light of selection.

When the monks of Mt. Hiei attacked Honen's ideas about the nembutsu in 1224, they claimed, "The Pure Land is the ultimate of all goodness and the nembutsu is a common discipline for all sects." During the Heian period the nembutsu was generally practiced along with other religious disciplines. From the various disciplines, Honen selected only one practice, that of recitation of the nembutsu, as the independent religious discipline necessary for salvation. The rest of the practices he classified as miscellaneous *(zogyo)* and assisting *(jogo)* disciplines.

Genshin (942-1017), one of the most influential Pure Land masters before Honen, declared that the nembutsu was the essential way of salvation. Besides the nembutsu, though, he also practiced and required assisting acts for fulfillment of Birth in the Pure Land. However, Honen explicitly stated his apprehension of the meaning of the nembutsu in this regard, "The Original Vow Nembutsu *(hongan nembutsu)* is independent. It does not need any assisting acts. If we think assisting acts are necessary for Birth, we will still be born at some distance from the Pure Land. The assisting disciplines may include developing wisdom, aspiration for enlightenment *(bodaishin)*, and compassion for others. Therefore, a good man practices the nembutsu as a good man and a bad man as a bad man. One should practice as he is. This practice is called the nembutsu without assisting disciplines." Thus, Honen emphasized the independent value of the nembutsu and labeled other good acts as assisting disciplines.

The nature of Honen's nembutsu as the "all inclusive" practice can be understood from the viewpoint of integration. In the *Senchaku-shu*, Honen presents the idea that the name of Amida Buddha is just like a house that comprises within it all its constituents such as the beams, rafters, pillars, verandah, and everything else used in the building. The name of Amida Buddha then has all other disciplines as parts of it. Even though he claims the importance of various Buddhist requirements, such as the threefold mind *(sanjin)* and the four modes of practice *(shishu)*, for devotees, he considers these disciplines, in the final analysis, to be integrated into the simple practice of the nembutsu. Thus Honen founded the teaching of the nembutsu as the ultimate way of religious salvation.

The Nembutsu as an Expression of Buddha Dharma

Self-understanding is essential for humans to realize their true nature. Ultimate transformation seems to be our major concern when the religious meaning of human existence is brought under examination. Significant change from illusion to truth, suffering to peace, ignorance to enlightenment, finite to infinite may be realized when one becomes perfectly aware of oneself and the world in which one lives. Religious teachings and practices are the means by which the change may be accomplished. The transformation may be achieved either individually or col-

lectively, in this life or in the next. In the Buddhist tradition there are at least two ways through which this transformation can be realized. One is the way of self-effort
(jiriki), in which man can attain enlightenment through the
practice of Buddhist teachings such as meditation and precepts. The other is the way of other power *(tariki)* of
Amida Buddha, by which one can attain Birth in the Pure
Land of Amida and become enlightened.

The nembutsu, one of the major religious practices in
Mahayana Buddhism, is considered to be a means of ultimate transformation, delivering man to the perfect state of
buddhahood. According to Honen, the nembutsu is the
recitation of the sacred name of Amida Buddha, *Namu
Amida Butsu*, and the ultimate religious discipline by
which man can be brought into the perfect realm of the
Buddha. In this way, the recitation of Amida's name is
regarded as the only way for devotees to attain salvation.
There have been, however, various other ways to practice
the nembutsu throughout the history of Buddhism.
Nembutsu is already found in earlier forms of Buddhism
to mean trust in Shakyamuni Buddha or reverence of his
virtues. Many Buddhist scriptures and masters have given
us various ways to practice the nembutsu. Some simply
enumerate them, and others try to show them in chrono-
logical order.

In searching for the meaning of the nembutsu as the
religious expression of Buddhist truth, we can find several
forms as follows:

*   *The nembutsu to attain ultimate oneness with the Buddha*

    This nembutsu sometimes refers to meditation on dharma-kaya, or the body of truth. In the profound state of concentration *(samadhi)*, one can experience being the Buddha and become aware of the true nature of buddhahood.

*   *The nembutsu to attain the experience of living with a buddha or living in the state of buddhahood*

    By meditating upon the image of a buddha, one can visualize a buddha in *samadhi* and thus realize Buddhist truth.

*   *The nembutsu to gain Birth in the Pure Land of Amida Buddha*

    This is closely related to the Original Vow of Amida. Amida Buddha's compassion, expressed in his vow to guide all beings to his land, is manifested through the recitation of the name. Therefore, the only discipline one should practice is to recite the name of Amida Buddha with faith in Amida's Original Vow. Thus the nembutsu is conceived as the expression of Buddhist truth in terms of great compassion *(mahakaruna)*. This is the type of nembutsu that Honen tried to present.

*   *The nembutsu as a gift of Amida Buddha*

In this teaching the nembutsu is not the way for man to gain Birth in the "Land of Buddha". It is the dynamic aspect of Buddha's power of wisdom and compassion. Amida himself participates in man's efforts in reciting the name. This represents Shinran's nembutsu.

These are some of the meanings of recitation in terms of the manifestation of truth. However, in studying the meaning of the nembutsu, we often assert that one form is the only way of expressing truth and others do not reveal it. It is sometimes stressed that Honen's nembutsu does not reveal Buddhist truth completely, but rather it is simply a stepping stone to Shinran's nembutsu. It is possible that Honen's nembutsu may be seen from a different angle or viewpoint such as Shinran's. The real meaning of Honen's nembutsu, however, should be properly examined and understood in the light of Honen's religious experience itself.

To explore the real meaning of Honen's nembutsu thought, we should take many factors into consideration such as his views on humanity and the social milieu of his time. However, here we are limited to the analysis of the inner structure of Honen's nembutsu as an expression of Buddhist truth. Before analyzing the structure, first we will examine the nature of Buddhist truth in order to establish a foundation for the discussion. Although Buddhist truth has been described in various terms, here it will be discussed in terms of wisdom (Skt. *prajna,* Jp. *chie*) and compassion (Skt. *karuna,* Jp. *jihi*), for these two are generally accepted as the key to understanding the nature of truth.

The Nature of Buddhist Truth

While *prajna* is essential, *karuna* may be considered as the concrete manifestation of truth. These are, however, not separate entities, but simply two aspects of one reality. Without *prajna*, there would be no real *karuna*; without *karuna* there would be no real *prajna*. *Karuna* is important when truth becomes particularly involved in the soteriological problems of humanity. This is because the majority of people need something concrete by which they can attain salvation. In the following pages we will discuss the nature of *prajna* and *karuna* briefly through the teachings of two leading Indian philosophers Nagarjuna (c.150-250) and Vasubandhu (c.400-480).

Wisdom *(prajna)* and Emptiness *(sunyata)*
Nagarjuna suggested *prajna* in terms of emptiness (Skt. *sunyata,* Jp. *ku*). According to his theory, every existence has meaning in relation to others. This principle is called dependent-origination (Skt. *pratitya-samutpada,* Jp. *engi*). In the *Mulamadhyamaka-karikas*, Nagarjuna critically observed the nature of existence in the world and concluded that going and goer, cause and effect, whole and parts, the senses, act and actor, desire and man, fire and fuel,

origination and disappearance, existence and non-exis-
tence, the aggregates, identity and difference, as well as
all the deepest doctrines of Buddhism - including suffering, the Tathagata, the Four Noble Truths, the chain of
causation, nirvana itself and so forth - all are mutually
dependent, and are conditioned by each other to exist.
Through the teaching of the *pratitya-samutpada*, he
proved that there is no self-existence, no thing-in-itself in
any existence.

Every existence is relative - relative not to some
absolute, but relative to each other. This indicates that the
reality of relative existence is denied and the duality of
subject and object is negated. Existence itself is regarded
as "nothing" or "empty" from the viewpoint of dependent-
origination, and the wisdom of non-dualism is thus
revealed. This is the wisdom of *sunyata*. This idea of non-
duality is found in the Eightfold Negation: There is no
production nor extinction, no annihilation nor perma-
nence, no unity nor diversity, no coming nor going. The
same sentiment is presented in many passages of the
Karikas.

Furthermore, in order to express the nature of existence as *sunyata*, Nagarjuna uses the negative dialectic:
the nature of existence is not "being", nor "non-being",
nor "either being or non-being", nor "neither being nor
non-being." This approach indicates that the negation of
the negation does not mean affirmation but progression to
higher truth. The highest truth is realized in the ultimate

state when every particular concept or theory is totally extinguished. If the denial is used as a denial against denial on the basis of mere metaphysical and conceptual argumentation, the true meaning of negation that is taught by Nagarjuna in order to express the ultimate nature of *prajna* will never be apprehended. This negative approach does not intend to create another theory or conceptual mode, but to provide the way for one to reach the state expressed as *sunyata*, which is beyond all modes of conception. Through this, we may realize that the negative dialectic is the means of apprehension of the ultimate nature of *sunyata*, which is the wisdom of non-duality or non-discrimination. Nagarjuna further reveals the true nature of *sunyata* as non-acquisition, which is attained after the extinction of all dogmatic, conceptual arguments. He also emphasizes that we should be free from all attachments and self-centeredness.

From this discussion, we may realize that the negative approach indicates the ultimate nature of *prajna* in terms of *sunyata*. This is attained in the domain beyond reason or intellect *(buddhi)* by re-moving the obstacles of dogmatic misconception. This is the expression of perfect wisdom attained when the cobwebs and clogs of narrow-minded thought-determination are completely eliminated. This is the supreme wisdom of non-discrimination which is beyond the limitation of a particular mode of thought or the discrimination of subject and object.

Compassion *(karuna)*

While *prajna* is the static aspect of Buddhist truth or buddhahood, *karuna* is the positive or dynamic aspect of buddhahood which is revealed in the phenomenal world. In
order to understand the meaning of *karuna* as the revelation of *prajna*, we turn to Vasubandhu. He developed the
contents of buddhahood on the basis of Nagarjuna's *sunyata* thought. That is, Vasubandhu positively interpreted the
nature of buddhahood in light of "being" and defined the
twofold wisdom, namely the wisdom of non-discrimination (Skt. *prajna,* Jp. *chie*) and the wisdom of the discrimination of non-discrimination (Skt. *jnana,* Jp. *chi*).

Regarding the nature of *prajna*, he stated that the ultimate nature of all beings (foolish, wise or enlightened) is
"empty," so that there is no discrimination or distinction
among them in their ultimate state. This is the same view
advocated by Nagarjuna.

Examining the contents further, Vasubandhu also
found another aspect of buddhahood. He presented this in
terms of "the nature of lubricating oil" which makes relationships among sentient beings smooth, and thereby
leads them into ultimate peace. In this regard, the nature of
buddhahood is expressed as *mahakaruna* (great compassion). This *mahakaruna* is based on *prajna* and is called
jnana. Jnana is the wisdom revealed in the finite world
and directed toward sentient beings, but it is not considered to be the wisdom or knowledge of finite beings.
Jnana implies the pure wisdom of non-discrimination

which manifests itself as a being or form in the finite world.

Since the wisdom of non-discrimination *(prajna)* is free from all mode of limitation and conditionality, it cannot be conceived of in our finite consciousness. Yet for the sake of finite beings, absolute wisdom manifests itself in the phenomenal world to bring every sentient being to the state of infinite, perfect wisdom. This manifested wisdom is called *jnana* and apprehended as *mahakaruna*. Thus we may conceive both *prajna* and *karuna* as two aspects of one reality, buddhahood. For this reason buddhahood is considered to have a dual character, having one foot in the infinite realm in terms of *prajna* and the other in the finite world in terms of *karuna*.

Regarding the relationship between *prajna* and *karuna*, Dr. Susumu Yamaguchi gives a detailed explanation by using the teaching of the Yogacara Consciousness-only school *(yuga-yuishiki)*:

The Supreme Emptiness, which transcends the discrimination of subject and object, works out as the being of non-being. Here the content of the supreme nature of Emptiness would be in two categories. One is non-being which transcends the discrimination between subject and object. The other is the being of non-being. These are not separate ones, but the latter is the complete form of the former. While the former is "emptiness" itself

which is realized after denying the argumentation
of subject and object matter, the latter is wisdom
(jnana) transformed from consciousness
(vijnana). This is the unique interpretation presented by the Yuga Yuishiki school. The former
means *sunyata* or *prajna*. The latter is not different
from the former in the point that both of them
contain the wisdom of non-discrimination *(sunyata)*, but it is different in the respect that *prajna*
works out as *jnana* (compassion or being of non-
being).

All this means that the ultimate nature of buddhahood
manifests itself through certain forms or modes, so that it
comes in contact with finite beings in worldly existence.
In this way, we sentient, finite beings can apprehend the
true nature of buddhahood through this form by which the
ultimate purpose of the Buddha (i.e., the liberation for all
or attainment of *prajna*) is accomplished. In this sense, the
Yuga Yuishiki school claims "the latter *(karuna)* is the
complete form of the former *(prajna)*." In this regard we
comprehend this form, being of non-being, as a "religious
manifestation of Buddhist truth" which has the function of
a mediator delivering one from the finite world to the infinite.

The Inner Structure of the Nembutsu
For Honen, the means of ultimate transformation deliver-

ing us from the finite into the infinite is the nembutsu. This is possible because it depends on the true nature of *karuna*. In Honen's teachings *karuna* is expressed in terms of Amida Buddha's Original Vow. The nembutsu is apprehended as the consummation of all the vows in Honen's declaration, "The vow of nembutsu must be the king of Amida's vows." An Original Vow (Skt. *purva-pranidhana*, Jp. *hongan*) is a strong wish or aspiration established by a bodhisattva in order to become a buddha. This Sanskrit term literally means "beforehand" *(purva)* and "to fix or focus on" *(pranidhana)*. Regarding the sacred vow of the bodhisattva there are two kinds: the general and the specific or original.

The general vow contains four objectives: (1) to liberate innumerable sentient beings, (2) to remove in-numerable defiled, passionate desires (Skt. *klesa*, Jp. *bonno*), (3) to learn an immeasurable amount of the teachings of the Buddha and (4) to attain enlightenment. The first vow is directed towards helping others attain enlightenment and the other three vows are for the attainment of enlightenment for one-self. This means that the religious aspiration of the bodhisattva in Mahayana Buddhism should first have the intention of liberating others. In order to accomplish this main purpose, s/he should engage in disciplines to eliminate the bondage of selfishness and to discover the reality of the universe.

On the other hand, the specific vow varies according to the bodhisattva. According to the *Sutra of*

Immeasurable Life, forty-eight vows are attributed to
Amida Buddha. These vows fulfilled by Amida are divided into three categories: vows by which to become a buddha, vows creating the Pure Land, and vows by which to
liberate all sentient beings. This means that the forty-eight
vows of Amida include Buddha's wisdom in order to
become an enlightened one and his compassion in order to
liberate all beings. Furthermore, when the nembutsu is
apprehended as the supreme vow, it is based on the
Buddha's compassion. That is to say, Amida provided the
vow of the nembutsu because it held the closest relationship to sentient beings without which salvation could not
be accomplished. The nembutsu thus becomes recognized
as a perfect manifestation of truth.

Inherent Nature

In analyzing the inner structure of the nembutsu presented
by Honen, we find two presuppositions. One is the inherent nature of the name of Amida, and the other is the practical value of the nembutsu itself. In regard to the former,
the true nature of buddhahood can be manifested through
the sacred name of Amida. This idea can also be seen
from two perspectives: one is the identity of name and
reality, the other is the all-inclusiveness of the name.

According to the principle of the identity of name and
reality, "name" is not merely a sound in the air but the revelation of reality itself. It has a mystical power to release
the inner property it represents when it is mentioned. This

type of name-cult can commonly be seen in the recitation of Vedic mantras, and in the name-taboo found in primitive man and modern man as well. Honen once said that the name of Amida had in its literal sense two virtues, infinite life and infinite light. The name Amida originally stems from *amitabha* (infinite light) and *amitayus* (infinite life) in Sanskrit. Thus Amida is considered to have the property of infinity within himself.

Furthermore, we can see that the name Amida is also regarded as an expression of truth in other schools. Amida is identical with the Threefold Truth of the Tendai school and the teaching of the character "A" as the ultimate source of existence *(A-ji Honpusho)* of the Shingon school. There are, however, fundamental differences between Honen and other schools. Honen said that Amida's name in this regard could be interpreted differently by each school and that his approach was not the way of perfect apprehension of the meaning inherent in the name, but the way of simple recitation of the name. It might be said that the way the Tendai school and the Shingon school took in understanding the name was "the way of wisdom," whereas the way Honen followed was "the way of compassion."

If Amida Buddha's name has supreme power because of its divine nature, then the name of all other buddhas would have the same power. If so, there is no reason for Honen to have chosen Amida only. He recognized that each buddha has the two vows of helping others to attain enlightenment *(rita)* and attaining enlightenment oneself *(jiri)*. However, he further said that no buddha but Amida could show the way of salvation for all through the name. He also said, "The Medicine Buddha (Skt. *Tathagata Bhaisajyaguru*, Jp. *Yakushi-nyorai*) established twelve vows but not the vow of universal salvation and the Thousand Armed Avalokitesvara (Skt. *Sahasrabhuj-aval-okitesvara Bodhisattva*, Jp. *Senju Kannon*) established the vow of universal salvation but has not fulfilled it yet. Only Amida established the vow of universal salvation and has already fulfilled it." Thus Honen was convinced that among the Buddhist divinities only Amida assures us of ultimate salvation.

In regard to the name, Honen also mentioned that the superiority of Amida's name to others is dependent on the inner virtues of "all-inclusiveness." He believed that the name "Amida" included all the virtues of Buddha. He understood the sacred name of Amida as the complete form which manifested itself through the accomplishment of the bodhisattva's vow. In the *Gyakushu Seppo("Pre-emptive Funeral" Sermons)*, Honen explains as follows:

> The excellent virtues of the name are that the
> Buddha reveals in the sacred name all the virtues
> of his cause and effect in general and in particular.
> Therefore, if we repeat the phrase *Namu Amida
> Butsu* even once, we will attain great benefit.

In the *Tozanjo*, he discusses the name in connection with the vow of nembutsu:

> He (Hozo Bosatsu), therefore, decided he would go through all possible austerities himself, however painful, through countless *kalpas* of time on their behalf and in their stead, and pile up the merit of myriad religious rigors so as to reach that perfect wisdom which would bring enlightenment to himself and to all sentient beings. Then concentrating in his own name every unfailing virtue, he would have all sentient beings appropriate the same by calling upon the sacred name, promising that whenever any would from their hearts so call on him, they would remember his vow and he would grant them Birth into his land.

The name of Amida represents buddhahood which is attained as the result of the fulfillment of a bodhisattva's vow. This is the realization of bodhisattvahood which contains the supreme wisdom of enlightenment and compassion to liberate all beings. The name, therefore, inherently embodies the supreme nature of the divine quality in the Buddhist tradition. Honen stated in the *Senchaku-shu*:

> The nembutsu is superior because all the virtues of Buddha are revealed in the name of Amida Buddha. Both Amida's inner virtues, such as the

four wisdoms, three bodies, ten powers, and four
kinds of fearlessness, and his external manifesta-
tions such as his glorified appearance, light,
words, and benevolence for others, all of Amida's
characteristics, are included in the name of
Amida. Therefore, the virtue of Amida Buddha's
name is superior to all others, because as they
make up only one part of the whole, they are infe-
rior to the nembutsu. This is like a house, for
example. The name "house" includes every part of
the structure: ridges, verandahs, and pillars. Yet
each of these parts does not and cannot include
the other parts of the house.

Thus he proclaimed that the name of Amida contained in
itself the perfect quality of buddhahood. Therefore in pre-
senting the absolute meaning of the nembutsu, Honen
suggests, "One nembutsu is unsurpassed," and "The devotee will attain Birth in the Pure Land by one repetition of
the nembutsu."

Here we should mention briefly the difference between
the nembutsu and the *dharani* (mystic syllables) of the
Shingon school. *Dharani* is also said to include various
virtues and teachings within itself. Therefore, as far as the
all-inclusiveness of the name or word is concerned, both
practices seem to be the same. Honen, however, explicitly
declared that *dharani* and the nembutsu are different in
that the latter is found in the Original Vow of Amida

whereas the former is not. Since the recitation of *dharani* demands concentration on its meaning and virtues, enlightenment may be realized through one's own effort of concentration and discipline. On the other hand, the concept of the divine name asserted by Honen is based on the Original Vow of Amida. It simply requests the recitation of the name with faith in Amida's Vow rather than difficult practices on the part of the devotee. The difference between the two depends on the different religious structure of each school.

Practical Value

First, let us inquire into how Honen tried to understand the teaching of the Buddha. There seem to be two approaches. One is that every word in the Buddhist scriptures and teachings must be the "golden" word of the Buddha. According to this view, the teaching of every denomination or school is true Buddhism. However, this is a superficial meaning of Buddhism. Though Honen once admitted all the teachings were Buddhism, he continued to ask himself whether or not people could accomplish these teachings proclaimed by each school. This consideration leads us to the second approach. Buddhism, if it is real, should be the way by which all beings can be liberated. The practical value of the nembutsu should be understood in this context, and thus closely related to the soteriological problem in Mahayana Buddhism.

What Honen was most concerned about was the teach-

ing of the Buddha which leads every sentient being to the
ultimate state of enlightenment. He emphasized that the
true meaning of Buddhism should be conceived not merely from the theoretical but from the practical side. In other
words, whether or not people can achieve this final goal
through the particular way that each denomination has
established is the critical factor for understanding the
meaning of the teaching of the Buddha.

At the discussion session held at Ohara in 1186,
Honen stated, "The Tendai school, the Shingon school, the
Kegon school, the Hosso school and the Sanron school
present their profound teachings, and all contain the same
supreme benefit. So if a devotee practices and fulfills all
the religious requirements, s/he will attain the profound
benefit of enlightenment." At the same discussion, it was
also said that the teaching of Pure Land Buddhism was as
good as the other doctrines. Honen, however, won the discussion regarding how to complete the teachings. He said
that no matter how excellent a teaching may be, if it is not
actually fulfilled because of the devotee's ability, vocation,
sex and so on, it should not be considered that which
reveals the truth of buddhahood. In this way, Honen was
deeply concerned about how Buddhism can actually be
put into practice.

This practical meaning of Buddhism is suggested in
Honen's thought in terms of "ease." In this context, he
found the meaning of the nembutsu as "easy to practice,
while all other disciplines are hard to practice." The term

"easy", however, does not imply "lazy", but rather it is the expression of ultimate concern. That is to say, the nembutsu represents the non-discriminatory nature of buddhahood which liberates all beings. From the basic thought of "easy," Honen reviewed Amida's Original Vow and described it as follows:

> If the making of statues and the erecting of pagodas were established as the Original Vow, then the poor and indigent must definitely relinquish their hope of Birth in the Pure Land. But the rich and noble are few and the poor and ignoble are extremely many. If great wisdom and superior abilities were established as the Original Vow, then the fool and the person of little knowledge must definitely relinquish their hope of Birth in the Pure Land. But the wise are few and the fools are extremely many. If the learning of many teachings was established as the Original Vow, then those who learn few must definitely relinquish their hope of Birth in the Pure Land. But those who learn few are extremely many and those who learn many are few. If the observance of precepts was established as the Original Vow, then those who violate the precepts must definitely relinquish their hope of Birth in the Pure Land. But those who observe the precepts are few and those who violate them are extremely many. The same

reasoning applies to all other practices.

In this manner, Honen apprehended Amida Buddha who, in his compassion for all sentient beings, did not vow to establish the making of statues or the erecting of pagodas as the condition for Birth in the Pure Land, but only the one act of reciting Amida's sacred name.

Genshin recognized the nembutsu as the central practice for attainment of Birth in the Pure Land. Yet he conceived of it in its highest sense as that practice to attain oneness with the supreme "emptiness." In the *Ojoyoshu* (*Collection on the Essentials for Birth*), Genshin understands the nembutsu to be an excellent way. However, according to Honen, the nembutsu of this kind could not fully reveal its real meaning, because not everyone can attain such a profound experience of oneness with the ultimate reality as Genshin or other devotees had attained. Thus Honen understood the true meaning of the nembutsu as the way of salvation for all. He said:

> The Pure Land denomination surpasses other denominations and the way of nembutsu is superior to other Buddhist disciplines because its teaching provides salvation for all kinds of people.

The meaning of the nembutsu as the way of salvation for all indicates the compassion *(karuna)*, the nature of buddhahood, through which the wisdom of non-discrimination *(prajna)* manifests itself in the finite world. Therefore in relation to the "ease" of the nembutsu, Honen explicitly stated:

> The nembutsu can be practiced by everyone because it is easy to do. Other disciplines cannot be practiced by everyone because they are too difficult. Therefore, by forsaking the difficult disciplines and taking up the easy one, Amida Buddha seems to have established the Original Vow of nembutsu for all classes of sentient beings so that they can attain, equally, Birth in the Pure Land.

He also gave a detailed explanation of this matter dealing with the Original Vow:

> The Original Vow means that Dharmakara Bodhisattva (Hozo-bosatsu) made forty-eight vows to Lokeshvararaja Buddha (Sejizaio-nyorai) before his becoming Amida Buddha a long time ago, in which he swore to create a purified buddha land and to liberate sentient beings into this land. Among these vows that Dharmakara Bodhisattva (Hozo-bosatsu) made, there is one called the vow of nembutsu by which all sentient beings would attain Birth in the Pure Land.

These indicate that through the nembutsu the infinite realization of Buddha's compassion is manifested.

In conclusion, in order to discuss the meaning of the nembutsu in relation to Honen's religious thought, we first examined the nature of Buddhist truth and found that *karuna* is the positive aspect of truth. Then we analyzed the inner structure of the nembutsu from two aspects the inherent nature of the name and its practical value. From the former, we have found that the name is the expression of truth because of its connection to the absolute. The name represents the totality of the reality named, thus Amida's name expresses the true nature of buddhahood. From the practical value of the name, we have realized that the nembutsu reveals the Buddhist truth in terms of *karuna*, because it is the solution of the soteriological problem in Buddhism. It is regarded as the ultimate way of salvation for all. In this way, it is made clear that the nembutsu is a religious expression of Buddhist truth.

Chapter Three

PURE LAND BUDDHISM

The Essence of Pure Land Buddhism

In the world there are many ideologies, systems of thought, and creeds by which we attempt to lead a better life or to realize an ideal society. Buddhism offers an excellent way for everyone to realize the ultimate goal of human existence in terms of "attaining enlightenment" through the profound awareness of truth.

According to Shakyamuni Buddha, final peace in the world as well as in the individual will be realized when the individual becomes liberated from ignorance and self-attachment, which are the causes of our suffering. Beyond the horizon of the finite, self-limited world, we can find the infinite world of great peace and happiness. When we learn and practice the teachings of the Buddha as presented in the scriptures, we will be able to attain this final state.

In the teachings of the Buddha, we can find many ways of realizing this final state. They may be classified into the two major streams: the Mahayana and the Theravada, the Esoteric and the Exoteric, the Easy Path and the Difficult Path, or Other-power and Self-power, respectively. According to the Pure Land tradition, the entire teaching of the Buddha can be divided into the twofold path of the Holy Way *(shodomon)* and the Pure Land *(jodomon)*.

The Holy Way is the way to attain enlightenment after eliminating ignorance and self-attachment by one's own effort. This may be called the way of wisdom, for it is the way to accomplish enlightenment by the power of wisdom attained through self-discipline. It is vitally important for a Buddhist to follow the teachings of the Buddha in order to achieve religious peace of mind. However, when observing our existential being seriously in the light of the way of wisdom, we often come to realize how much we are unable to fulfill the required disciplines to eliminate ignorance and self-attachment. The more we seriously reflect upon ourselves, the more we may find ourselves "unliberated" by the way of wisdom.

When we lose the way to enlightenment by the Holy Way, we often sink down into a world of darkness and despair. Amida Buddha, however, provides a way for us to attain salvation from this hopeless state. This is the way

illuminated by the light of the grace of Amida Buddha, the
Path to the Pure Land. The Pure Land school opens the
channel to attain salvation for those unliberated through
the way of wisdom. However, since this school is different
from the Holy Path, it is sometimes referred to as pseudo-
Buddhism. It seems to be Buddhism, but it is not considered to be genuine from the traditional point of view. Pure
Land Buddhism is also mistakenly regarded as a religion
for lazy people. It is sometimes called the Easy Path as it
requires only the simple act of faith and recitation of the
nembutsu as its primary religious disciplines rather than
the many practices of observing precepts, attaining the
state of "emptiness," chanting the various sutras and so
forth, as the means of reaching enlightenment.

The Pure Land school established on this basis may be
called the way of salvation by a "power outside of ourselves," or "other power" (i.e., the power of Amida
Buddha). Buddhism is the teaching of the Buddha and the
teaching by which to become a buddha, that is, Buddhism
is the way through which everyone, regardless of age, sex,
race, or ability can be liberated and attain enlightenment.
Therefore, if anyone of disability were excluded it could
not be considered Buddhism in its true sense. In other
words, Buddhism cannot reveal its truth if anyone is eliminated. When Buddhism is understood as the way of universal salvation, we can understand the profound meaning
of the Pure Land school. The essence of Pure Land
Buddhism is revealed and apprehended through this line

of reasoning and belief.

The Compassion of Amida Buddha

However simple a thing may appear, it may inherently contain many elements that keep it as it is. For instance, we generally think of a stone or a piece of board as a "solid" thing. According to modern physics, however, a solid thing may be conceived of as a whirling mass of electrical charges. Every object keeps its shape and function by a complex relationship among the elements that constitute it.

Behind the success of any great actor or actress on the stage or on the screen, there are hundreds and thousands of unknown people working "behind the curtain." The cooperation and integrity of these people are important factors in the success of the performer. Observing any family through the backdoor, we may find there to be much distress, many troubles, large or small, that cannot be seen or perceived from the front entrance by an outsider. We know that an unexpected crisis may occur even in a peaceful family.

We believe that the home is a place where all members of a family can come together and relax from the cares and worries of the world outside. However, in actual life, we encounter many problems in the family itself. In order to solve these problems and preserve peace within the family, we need deep understanding and cooperation among the members of the family. But this is not as easy to do as to say.

We see a duck swimming smoothly on the surface of the water, but we may often miss the fact that he is constantly moving his legs under the water. His smooth movement on the surface is engineered by his legs hidden in the water. In order to have a family that gets along smoothly and peacefully, each one of us must make a great effort, perhaps behind the scenes, to keep it as we wish.

A book on Chinese philosophy called the *Saikontan* states, "Although the world is essentially large, greediness makes it small." The world in truth should be beyond that which is individually confined or limited. The world in truth is the place in which people can freely and peacefully live together. However, this world that is supposed to be large will become small when each individual merely concerns himself with his own interests alone.

The Buddha teaches us that it is important to avoid narrow-mindedness and selfish interests in order that we may live in a world of peace and happiness. Narrow-mindedness may be evoked when we think that each of us can live by ourselves alone, without any relation to others. The Buddha taught that we should see the reality of ourselves as the totality of innumerable forces of life; that is, we only maintain life, even for a moment, as a result of innumerable blessings.

Seeing a flower gives us a pleasant feeling. Sometimes it helps us be relieved from tension. Sometimes it leads us into the world of beauty. For a flower to fulfill its life cycle, there must be roots under the ground that we do not readily see. The roots support the tree and give it nourishment through numerous sub-roots which help the tree to grow and produce beautiful flowers. Invisible from the surface and stepped on by everyone, the roots work patiently for just a single flower. Without these roots, the flower could not display its beauty and fulfill its life cycle.

For us to live even for a moment, there must exist the invisible force of blessings just as the stem of a flower has its hidden roots beneath the ground. This is the force of dependent origination *(pratitya-samutpada)*. When this force is religiously apprehended, we may say that it is Amida Buddha who continuously gives us life in the present as well as in the eternal future.

The human effort to apprehend the reality of the invisible force of Amida Buddha is stated in Honen's poem:

> There is no place the moon does not shine,
> But it only illuminates
> in the heart of those who gaze at it.

Regardless of our awareness, the grace of the Buddha is always with us. This is the great compassion and love of Amida Buddha that is beyond the reach of our apprehension. Honen reveals the truth of this great blessing of the Buddha through the teaching of the nembutsu.

God and Amida Buddha

The most important thing for us to understand Buddhism is the fact that Shakyamuni, a human being, awakened to truth and became the Buddha. We discussed the three-bodies of Buddha *(trikaya)* previously. This was an expression of the insight of Shakyamuni's enlightenment. The fact that Shakyamuni became a buddha means that every human being can become a buddha. The Mahayana tradition strongly emphasizes that every sentient being has buddha-nature (Skt. *buddhata*, Jp. *bussho*). We have buddha-nature within ourselves. A buddha and an ordinary person are ultimately the same by nature, the same ontologically. The only difference is the degree of apprehension of truth. A buddha has attained perfect wisdom, but we sentient beings have not yet attained it. That is, a buddha and an ordinary person differ from each other epistemologically.

On the other hand the Christian God has a different nature from Buddha. God is the creator of the universe, the absolute existence, the highest being, etc. God is quite different from man. He is the creator and man is the created. God is perfect good and man is a sinner. Man cannot become God however hard he may try. God and man are totally different from each other by nature, different ontologically. While God is perfect truth, man cannot attain the perfect truth of God. God is far from us. He is beyond our apprehension. God and man differ from each other epistemologically.

Thus the difference between God and Buddha in relation to man would be as follows: God is different from
man epistemologically and ontologically, whereas Buddha
is different from man epistemologically but not ontologically.

However, when we come to Pure Land Buddhism, God
and Amida Buddha seem to be the same. Both are
believed in as a savior by devotees. Among the branches
of Buddhism, the Pure Land school particularly emphasizes "faith." Devotees of the school realize that they do
not attain enlightenment by their own power, but by simply having faith in Amida's power of salvation.

We have buddha-nature within ourselves but we cannot reveal its true nature by ourselves. Its revelation is
achieved only by Amida's grace. Our salvation is entirely
dependent upon Amida Buddha. Thus as far as this aspect
of Amida as a savior is concerned, we may see that Amida
and God appear to be the same, but Amida also has a different aspect from that of God. Amida Buddha is not the
creator or ground of all being.

According to the *Sutra of Immeasurable Life*, Amida
Buddha is described as follows. Many eons ago there was
a king. He had the opportunity to listen to a sermon given
by a buddha, Tathagata Lokeshvararaja (Sejizaio-nyorai).
Upon hearing the sermon, he made up his mind to
renounce his palace life, and he became a monk called
Bodhisattva Dharmakara (Hozo-bosatsu). He established

forty-eight vows as a Bodhisattva and practiced austere
religious disciplines for a long time. He accomplished
these vows and became the Buddha called Amitabha.
Among the forty-eight vows, the eighteenth vow is the
vow of the nembutsu through which every man can attain
salvation.

Now you may notice that Amida was a man and
became a buddha. He is not the creator nor an absolute
being, but his prolonged religious practices made him a
great savior of the world. This indicates that he does not
belong to the domain of God but to that of Buddha. He is
within the range of Buddhist divinity

Furthermore, the story of Amida's enlightenment
reflects the life of Shakyamuni. This means that Amida
Buddha is the symbolic expression of the ultimate nature
of Shakyamuni Buddha. He is the great liberator of the
world and the great source of all life. Once again, God and
Amida Buddha are both considered great saviors of the
world.

The Meaning of "Pure Land"

Meaning of the Description in the Scriptures
The Pure Land is the land of Amida Buddha, the final
goal of Pure Land Buddhism. The description of the Pure
Land differs from scripture to scripture. According to the
Amida Sutra (Skt. Smaller *Sukhavativyuha Sutra*, Jp.
Amida-kyo), one of the main sutras of Pure Land

Buddhism, the Pure Land is described in terms of *goku-raku* (paradise) as follows:

> In *gokuraku*, the Realm of Supreme Bliss, there is
> a pond made of seven jewels, which is filled with
> the pure, crystalline water of the eight virtues. The
> bottom of the pond is covered with golden sand.
> On the edge of the pond there is a beautiful build-
> ing of several stories which is composed of gold,
> silver, emeralds and crystal. In the pond, wheel-
> sized lotus flowers bloom with blue flowers emit-
> ting blue light, yellow flowers emitting yellow
> light, red flowers emitting red light, and white
> flowers emitting white light. They give forth a
> wonderful fragrance around the pond.

Some of those who hear or read this description in the sutra may think that this is just an old-fashioned fairy tale to be enjoyed by childish minds. Some psychologists may say this is not a real world but simply a fantasy created by a frustrated mind trying to escape from the realities of the suffering and unhappiness of life in this world. It may also be claimed that this is a world of illusion produced by thoughts of selfish and blind desire or mere imagination.

To counter this severe challenge from the modern mind, there have been many attempts to understand the true meaning of this description. First, the Pure Land does not belong to our present world, but to the "other" world

which comes after death. Since no one has returned from
the other world and talked about it to us, from the empiri-
cal viewpoint there seems no reason to affirm the existence of the Pure Land in the next world. Yet at the same
time, there is no sound reason to deny it. From a profound,
reflective viewpoint or religious standpoint, we may
understand the various meanings of the future.

Secondly, the Pure Land is a world which exists
beyond our realm of concepts. Since we are living in a
world hemmed in by our limited faculties of perception,
our area of understanding is restricted. It is hard to understand others perfectly. It is even difficult to comprehend
our own self. The Pure Land, therefore, cannot be fully
comprehended if we ourselves do not actually experience
it. Whether it is real or unreal is beyond the realm of argument.

Thirdly, the Pure Land is understood as the ideal world
that shall be established on this earth some day. Tokugawa
Ieyasu, the founder of the Tokugawa feudal government in
Japan (1600-1868), was influenced by Pure Land
Buddhism. When he went to the battlefield, he carried a
banner with him bearing the famous motto: "Denying the
impure world, seeking the Pure Land." He is considered to
have made an attempt to establish the Pure Land on this
earth.

Fourthly, the description of the Pure Land is a material
expression of Buddhist truth, i.e., the expression of man's
enlightenment to the universal truth. This is the state of

absolute value to be revealed when man awakens to the truth of existence.

Fifthly, the Pure Land is the state of buddhahood. According to Honen, the Pure Land is the state of the realization of Amida's Original Vow. It is the state in which Amida Buddha's wisdom and compassion are manifested. Therefore, it is sometimes described as the eternal world. It is also sometimes described as a world of peace and harmony.

Spontaneity

In order to understand further the meaning of the Pure Land, let us look again at the *Amida Sutra*, where we come across the following passage:

> In the "Land of Buddha", we have soft breezes and hear beautiful sounds of bells among the trees. This is just like a great symphony which is played by hundreds and thousands of instruments at the same time. Upon hearing this sound of music, everyone spontaneously realizes the meaning of the three treasures of Buddha, Dharma and Sangha.

Elsewhere in the sutra, it is also stated that all seven jewels are created spontaneously. Sometimes it is described how the inexpressible beauty and virtues of the Pure Land are produced by the spontaneous or natural act of being. What does "spontaneity" or "naturalness" mean in terms of the Pure Land?

One day a Zen master pointed out a crooked pine tree in the temple precincts and asked his disciples how they could see it correctly. One answered that they could measure it. The second said that he could see it correctly by chopping the tree into pieces and analyzing it. Another suggested that they should see it as a straight tree, for the pine tree was crooked due to external forces. Many other ideas were brought under argument. Concluding the discussion, the Zen master said, "The right way to see the tree is not to see it as a straight tree nor to analyze it, but rather to see it as it is." To see the object "as it is" is an important matter for us to bear in mind. This approach to apprehension is expressed in Buddhist literature by such terms as "spontaneity" or "naturalness." However, when these terms come to be used in an ordinary sense, they are often misleading.

These terms do not refer to impulsive acts or selfish conduct for fulfilling one's desires. For example, when one goes to a department store or market, one sees in the show windows or on the shelves many things which are as beautiful and attractive as one would want. If one were to follow the natural sequence of the desire to possess them, though one may not have enough money to buy them, one could end up unconsciously stealing the things one wanted. If a man, seeing an attractive and charming woman, were to obey the order of natural, impulsive desire, what would happen?

The spontaneous act or natural response used to express the nature of the Pure Land does not belong to this category of the term, that is, an impulsive or instinctive act to fulfill one's desires. The state of being implied by the term "naturalness" is that of "unconsciousness," though again this does not mean the unconscious behavior of humans to satisfy selfish and blind urges. The "unconscious" state here refers to the original state or the state before the conscious act appears.

When we see something through red glasses, we see it as a reddish object. Seeing it through blue glasses, we perceive the object in blue. In reality, however, the object is neither red nor blue. Because of "colored glasses", we often distort the true facts so that we do not see things correctly. In conscious life it is exactly the same. By viewing an object through colored glasses, we cannot grasp its real aspect. The unconscious realm means seeing the object as it is, or to perceive or conceive of the true nature of things as they are. This is the state without the "colored glasses" of selfish desire, or the state before putting them on.

We often hear people criticizing other people and various aspects about them. Actually it is very hard to get to the genuine nature of the individual unless we see or hear him without any "colored glasses" of prejudice or biased knowledge. We are in a deceptive state of mind through these "glasses" of self-centeredness. Because of this deceptive state of mind, we cannot see the real nature of things.

The Realm of Eternal Life

The sun gives us all its light and heat without making any distinctions between individuals. Water is given to us all, man and woman, good and bad, alike.

We ourselves, or things that we think are ours, are not our own but are the body or things that have been brought about by the blessings of the "Great Life" of Amida which works without discriminating between color, creed, or nationality anywhere in the universe. What you are and what I am are simply the fruit of the "Great Life" which is brought about by non-discriminating compassion and love of all things.

Therefore, in accordance with this "Great Life", we are not limited in life but are to live in eternal life. This is the manifestation of the original nature, the "natural and spon-taneous act" of being. Thus the Pure Land, our final goal, is the state of naturalness or spontaneity, which is not an illusory world produced by our selfish desires, not one created by a childish mind, but is rather a world in which every being, tree, flower or pond exists as it is, and in which we live as we are.

This is the realm of eternal life and light, for it is beyond the limited world bound by selfish desires. This is the world of purity because of the realization of the pure or original nature of being. This is the world of oneness, oneness with others. This is the "Land of Buddha" in which every one lives as s/he is, together with others peacefully and harmoniously.

Location

It is said that an astronaut of the Soviet Union once gave his impression of his trip into space as follows: "However high I might go up in the sky, I could not see the Heaven which had been taught by religion." This may reflect the mind of one who adheres to a materialistic way of thinking, and who denies the existence of God and Heaven. This may also be the view held by many people in this modern age.

If the term "heaven" is conceived as a realm situated somewhere in the sky, any religion that had such an idea would become unintelligible to those modern minds who attempt to comprehend the matter through merely materialistic and scientific rationality. For them it would belong to the pre-modern world.

It is true that in the sacred scriptures of various religions we can find many fantastic and wonderful descriptions of this ultimate state. In regard to the Pure Land, we have already seen the inexpressible spectacle of this Buddha Land. The scriptures of Pure Land Buddhism also deal with the location of the Pure Land. It is stated that the Pure Land is located millions of countries away towards the West. We are told that the Buddha Land of supreme beauty and happiness, to which we will be Born after death, is remote.

Two things should be mentioned here. One is the matter of the direction "West" and the other is that of the distance to the Buddha Land. The "West" in this context signifies the final destination of human life. Ancient people believed that just as the sun set in the west, so would we be born in the western world when we terminated our lives. Thus the term "West" refers not only to a geographical location but also symbolizes man's final state.

As for the distance to the Buddha Land, we come across another description in the *Meditation Sutra*, "Amida Buddha is not far from here. Therefore one should see the Buddha's Land through meditation." Sometimes it is also said that this world of birth and death is identical with the Pure Land of peace and brightness. At this point we may get confused because the Pure Land is presented in two contradictory ways. On the one hand, it is described as being situated at an unimaginable distance from here, and on the other hand, it is said to be located right here in our present life. What does this mean? What is the Buddha's real intention?

The way the Pure Land is described in a contradictory manner indicates that the matter of peace or happiness depends on the individual. The state of happiness or the Pure Land is near at hand for those who are enlightened to truth, but it may be far away for those who are not enlightened.

An old proverb states that it is difficult to gather one thousand pieces of gold, yet it gives unforgettable pleasure when just a little goodwill is shown or a glass of water is received. It is not easy to earn a thousand dollars, but we may sometimes not feel gratitude to those who would give it to us. However, we may feel profound gratitude to those who give us just a cup of milk. This indicates that the world that one lives in differs according to the way one's mind responds. The decisive thing is not the material things one receives. It is great to thank someone for even a tiny thing, while it is sad to forget to appreciate the receipt of a great amount of things. Thanksgiving is the source of happiness and harmony.

Oneness
Parents and children, husband and wife, brothers and sisters, who all live together under one roof, may not live peacefully and happily when they cannot communicate and understand one another. The home, which is supposed to be the center of a happy life, may become unpleasant. We may see many troubles and a cold atmosphere in a family supposed to be happy because of its material wealth. On the contrary, we also know that there are families, although poor materially, in which we can feel much warmth and affection because of profound understanding and cooperation.

If we do not have perfect communication between parents and children, we feel like strangers rather than parents and children, and thus we go out into a cold, lonely world. I have heard of a young man who had done something wrong and was held by the police. When his father got this bad news, he went to the police station immediately where his son was detained. After the proper procedures, his son was released. The son, who came out and met his father, said, "Dad, what happened to you? You don't have to pay my bond. You don't have to waste money on me. I will be free when I finish may term in jail." Thinking of his son's future, the father made every effort to raise the money for his son's bail. However, this boy could not understand his father's deep feeling and affection. Furthermore, he seemed to have wanted for himself the money that his father had used for his own release. This is a very sad state of affairs in the relationship between parent and child.

This kind of incident, however, is not restricted to the relationship between parents and child, but can occur in any human relationship throughout our lives, such as between man and woman, husband and wife, brothers and sisters, friends and members in the community. Lack of communication and understanding often drive people into a miserable state.

We sometimes have to live apart from other members of the family. During war, a young son may be dispatched to a battlefield a long distance away from his country. A young man may sometimes be sent to a college to study far away from his home town. However, even if parents and children live hundreds or thousands of miles away from each other, when parents pray for a child's success in work and for her happiness, and when the child prays for the happiness and good health of her parents, there is a realm of oneness in their hearts. Physically they may be far away from each other, but spiritually they are one.

Among parents who think deeply of their children and children who are aware of the profound love and affection of their parents, there is a great world of peace and happiness which is beyond the limitations of time and space. The Pure Land is a world of oneness, a world of happiness and peace filled with brightness and a wealth of beauty. This is understood by the mind aware of truth that is beyond time and space. This is the world of Buddha where everyone can meet and live together happily and forever.

Purity

When we come to a river and try to see an object in the water, we cannot see the thing clearly if the water is muddy. We may argue about the thing in the water. One may say it must be a fish; another says it must be a rock; still others say it must be a piece of wood. The argument will continue without reaching the right answer. However, when the water becomes clear and pure, we can clearly see the object in the water as it truly is. Thus we can reach the right answer and consequently the argument will cease.

As we observe our human life, there may befall some unavoidable unhappiness or trouble because of a slight misunderstanding. Shakyamuni Buddha always warned that when we are in the bonds of the narrow-minded, self-determined world, we may easily assert ourselves to be right and consequently label others as wrong. One dark night, a boy came back home from visiting a friend of his. On the way, he had to pass through a forest. He felt alone and scared. In the middle of the forest, he suddenly saw a big snake. He froze and then fainted in fear. His mother became worried by his lateness and came looking for him. In the forest, she found him on the ground near a big rope. She stirred him and asked why he had fallen down. He told her the whole story that he had seen a big snake. However, when he realized that it wasn't a snake but simply a piece of rope, he was relieved and happy. A frightened mind and preconceptions made him scared, but a clear mind and proper perception brought him a happy and relieved state of mind.

When we are interested in ourselves alone, we easily lose sight of the greater world of truth and so we may fall into a state of hell and suffering. Therefore, we should carefully reflect upon ourselves imprisoned in ignorance and self-attachment. When we have eliminated these elements of impurity (ignorance and self-attachment), we naturally enter a world of purity and brightness. In this state, there are no silly arguments nor any misunderstandings among people. Everything is conceived "as it is" without any distortion that may occur because of self-attachment and ignorance. This is the state of being a buddha and is called the Pure Land. The Pure Land is thus the state in which one can see things with "pure" or "correct"

perception brought about by the elimination of impurity.
This state is apprehended as one where there is no suffering nor sorrow and only happiness and peace.

Chapter Four

ESSENTIAL BUDDHISM

Interdependence

One of the important ways to understand what Buddhism is involves considering the question: "What is the essential system of thought in Buddhism by which we can properly see the things that exist around us and by which we can correctly understand what human life is and what the universe is?"

The word that manifests and indicates the fundamental spirit of Buddha's enlightenment is "interdependent causation" or "dependent origination" (*pratitya-samutpada*). It is important for a Buddhist to apprehend the true knowledge of "dependent origination." To clarify the meaning of this vital word, I would like, by way of illustration, to employ a very familiar example that can be found in our surroundings.

Suppose here we have the seed of a peach. This is a good seed and has within itself the power to grow well. Yet do you think that this seed can grow by itself? Of course not. As all of us know, there are many elements or factors which help the seed grow: the ground and soil give it a place to sprout, water gives it moisture, sunshine gives it heat, fertilizer gives it nourishment, and even human hands take care of it. There are even other factors as well that contribute to its growth. Thus in order for a single seed to grow, there must be proper interaction among all these elements.

Furthermore, even though a seed has all the necessary things for its growth, if there is no balance among them, the seed cannot grow correctly. It needs water but if there is too much water the seed will rot. It needs the sun's heat but if the sunlight is too strong, the seed will die, and so on. Thinking in this way, we realize that many things are working together interdependently and harmoniously for one seed to grow. In order for the seed of a peach to grow into a tree, producing beautiful blossoms and bearing fruit, many vital elements are necessary. Thus we now see that behind the beautiful appearance of peach blossoms, there are many things that act together, helping one another and relating to each other to cause the growth of a tiny seed. In seeing and tasting even one peach, we can realize the blessing that is created and is the result of the interdependent activities of various energies and factors.

In this manner, when enjoying flowers in the garden, blossoms in a tree, or various trees standing in a park, we can see the state of harmony and glory that manifests the spirit of *pratitya-samutpada*, the profound thought of dependent origination. Accordingly everything, living or non-living, is able to exist because of its relationship with other things and beings. Everything must be related to everything else in order to exist. There is nothing in this world that is not related to other things. There is nothing that exists independently. Everything in this world, every one of us, is related to each other in some way or another. This is the profound spirit of *pratitya-samutpada*.

Now let us think of our lives in light of this "dependent origination." Can we live by ourselves alone? Of course not. Most people know that we need many things in order to live in the world, and that we are being helped from the outside by other persons and other things. We sometimes, however, misconceive of our human lives and think that we are living by ourselves alone. Thus we come to behave selfishly and indifferently to others. This way of understanding human life is quite opposite to the essential thought of Buddhism. This kind of thinking may put our entire lives into a state of disorderliness, chaos and unhappiness. We human beings are not perfect. We may make mistakes, but at the same time, we should realize that we have the faculty to reflect upon ourselves and upon what we have done. Knowing this, we should try to improve ourselves. In the course of human affairs what we should bear in mind is to share each other's views and ideas, to help one another, and to understand each other so that we may grow spiritually.

The matter of growth or maturity has two aspects. One is physical, the other spiritual. We can grow physically more easily than spiritually. In order to become mature spiritually, we must make a great effort. It is not easy to do this, but we should do it as much as is humanly possible. Some of us may notice that there are people who have grown up physically but not spiritually.

When we contemplate our lives, we may realize that first we must have parents, a father and a mother, to be born into this world. Particularly in the period of infancy, children need to be well cared for by parents. In the process of growing up, we are influenced not only by parents but also by friends, teachers and many other people, through whom we learn all kinds of things - some good and some bad.

Furthermore, besides these human elements, we also see many other non-human factors. As for the physical body, we need air, water and salt, food and heat and many other things to keep the body healthy. Studying the human body, scientists and medical doctors show us that there are many elements and organisms that make up the body. These elements are related to each other and act together to maintain balance and harmony among themselves to keep our health good. If this balance is upset, then we find ourselves in a state of ill health. If we realize that we are healthy now, we should awaken to the fact that we are in a state of blessedness that has been created and given by the interdependent, harmonious activities that are the basis of human existence.

When we think about our spiritual growth as well as our physical growth, we find more things that surround us. Mountains, rivers, flowers, grass by the road, trees - all these things convey some kind of significance and meaning to our lives. All these things evoke a pleasant feeling in our minds, and enrich our spiritual lives; thus they assist us in creating human culture.

Considering ourselves in this manner, we may realize that our lives are in a great state of blessing that is pro-created by the interdependent acts among various countless elements and conditions. We are not living by ourselves alone, but rather we are living by virtue of the great power of blessings which fill heaven and earth. In this way, the answer to the question, "What is the basic thought of Buddhism?", is *pratitya-samutpada*, "dependent origination." Everything in the world is interrelated to every other thing in one way or another. Through these dynamic activities, we have been able to live, are kept alive, and will continue to live. We may say that we exist because of the help of other persons and also because of the outside influence of many other things, living and non-living. In a way, each individual manifests this total unity. From this fundamental thought, Buddhist philosophy, literature, culture, and general heritage have been created.

Impermanence

The late Abbot Zenkei Shibayama of Nanzen-ji temple in Kyoto wrote a beautiful poem.

> A flower blooms in silence, falls in silence,
> And never returns to its stem.
> In a moment, at just one place,
> It forgoes all its life.
> The voice of a flower,
> the reality of the flower stem.
> There the happiness of eternal life
> is shining without regret.

After a severe, cold winter, when spring comes, nature becomes colorful and bright. We feel the invisible force behind the budding and growing of even one small flower in the garden and of a blossom on a tree. The world is open and has awakened with dynamic vitality from its prolonged sleep of winter just past. All the flowers and blossoms decorate our world. We enjoy seeing and appreciating them. We sense new life in the trees and the woods. We feel a great energy to grow and to live into the promised future. From ancient times, it is said that youth is the flower of the world.

The tree, however, cannot hold the blossom forever. The flowers, whether beautiful or ugly, will wither and fall. The beautiful world of blossoming comes to an end.

Observing this succession of life in the natural world, the end of life on earth, we might come to feel lonesome and sad. The end of life which is death is an inevitable fact to every being. Not only flowers but also human beings cannot escape from this stern reality of life.

Shakyamuni Buddha teaches us that change is the basic truth of existence. Every moment of life is different from every other moment. Everything is changing forever. Life is a continuation of the moment. Every being is in flux. Every moment is birth and death. Where there is birth, there is death. Where there is death there is birth. Thus we are in a state of dynamic "becoming of life." This is the teaching of Impermanence (Skt. *anitya*, Jp. *mujo*).

The cherry blossom is one of the most beautiful flowers in the world. Everyone enjoys seeing it, but by even a short gust of wind or rain during the night, it will fall. It cannot stay in the same state even for a moment.

In the simple life of the flower, blooming and falling, we discover the truth of life. The flower blooms in this world without intending to make people feel bright and happy or leading them into unhappiness and sadness; the flower blooms simply to fulfill its essential nature and the virtue of blooming. It will disappear when its time comes. There is no intention or purpose to give appreciation to people who enjoy or benefit from it. When we realize that a flower blooms just for a moment, it gives us something of eternal value. We can see there eternal life and eternal happiness. Though the flower has no voice to talk to us with, it may convey the meaning and significance of living, and we may hear the voice of voicelessness. When we listen to the voiceless voice of the flower, we may realize how valuable and important it is to live for the moment in fulfilling one's own nature. As there is eternal life in a moment of the blossom, so do we strive to realize the eternal wisdom in the "moment" of our life.

Not-Self

Another important concept in Buddhism is Not-Self (Skt. *an-atman*, Jp. *mu-ga*). "Self" in this context refers to one absolute eternal Substance. The ancient Hindu tradition admitted the existence of Self as Absolute Substance. Self in us is similar to the soul which is the source of man's transmigration. Self primarily implies the Absolute Self in us but later on it also implies any absolute entity. The reason why Buddhism denies Self is that it understands every existence in the world to be a simple state of cooperative activities of many factors. Not-Self is another expression of *pratitya-samutpada*, dependent origination.

In America, there are many beautiful rose gardens. We enjoy looking at their various colors and smelling their fragrance. And we wonder where such beauty comes from. Does it come from the center of the stem or the root under the ground, or the twig holding the flower? We cannot see the substance of the flower's beauty within itself. We comprehend its beauty as the totality of the rose tree.

The roses are the fruit of the cooperative activity of various factors of the tree. They are not something that has grown from one substance alone.

The house we live in is not built of one substance. It comprises many parts such as pillars, beams, windows, floor and so on. Since it is not a structure of eternal substance, it will grow weak and break down into parts, and then disappear as time elapses.

Physics shows that many elements put together harmoniously can create new things. We cannot see a beautiful rose in the stem or in the twig, but the whole rose tree creates a new thing which is a rose. Pillars, beams and floor are not a house, but when they are properly constructed together they are transformed into a new thing called a house.

Mentally, we human beings are prone to becoming attached to our own created image of thought and to be imprisoned by it. We live in the small world of Self and lose sight of apprehending the true nature of things. In our communication, we need to go beyond our narrowly self-confined realm and come into the realm of others. Real communication takes place when we can identify with each other in this way.

The concept of Not-Self can also be described in connection with art. Sir Herbert Read, a British critic of art and literature who has some knowledge of Zen Buddhism, once said that art and religion were deeply related to each other in Zen. He illustrated an interesting Zen anecdote.

When an artist tries to draw a bamboo he "should draw a bamboo for ten years, become a bamboo, and then forget about bamboo when he is drawing a bamboo." "To become a bamboo and forget about it" are important points. A real bamboo may be drawn when the artist identifies himself with the rhythm of the bamboo while drawing. The Buddhist training of Not-Self in Zen is the way of attaining "the rhythmic movement of the spirit" which is vital to a good artist.

Nagarjuna tells us that "emptiness" (*sunyata*) is the state of truth, but warns us that when we attach to it, it will no longer be *sunyata*. Attachment causes *sunyata* to lose its true nature. Real *sunyata* as truth is the state of complete non-attachment to Self. Negatively, the teaching of Not-Self shows us that we should forsake every self-attachment; positively, it implies the great compassion and love that a buddha extends to every one of us.

Emptiness

One of the characteristic teachings of Buddhism is expressed as "emptiness" or "nothingness." The term "emptiness" used in this context does not mean that life is empty and has no meaning. Rather, it indicates the supreme state of human spirituality which is the source of happiness and peace. "Emptiness" is a word that indicates the state of oneness that is beyond the discrimination brought about by human self-attachment. Its positive meaning is the realization of the full meaning of existence or the desire to live our lives to the fullest extent.

We human beings often encounter much physical and spiritual suffering. Of these, it is most dreadful and unfortunate if there is a lack of understanding between the members of a family, because the family is the basic unit of our lives and the source of our security and happiness.

When our minds do not respond to the other's mind naturally, when we do not understand each other correctly, there is a sad feeling in our hearts, even in the closest relationships - such as those between parents and children, or even husbands and wives.

When things go along as well as we expect them to, it is difficult to understand the meaning of suffering, and we even forget to pay attention to minor unpleasant things. When we are in good health, we are prone not to think of sickness. Therefore, if we come upon an unexpected or dreadful situation, we may complain, "Why should I have such terrible luck?" In such a case, we may forget what we have done and even try to blame others for the unpleasant conditions that have occurred.

When we are in good condition physically, mentally, and financially, we are inclined to think as if we were living unto ourselves, individually and independently, and prefer not to be bothered with other people. However, when we are alone or when everyone goes away from us, we become sad and lonely.

If we believe, however, that the body of an individual

is complete in itself, as we often tend to think, there is no reason why we have to experience loneliness when we become separated from our loved ones by death or for other reasons. The fact that we do experience such loneliness indicates that one's life does not exist independently, but is created in dynamic relationship with others.

Though we are apart from each other physically, there is a realm within our hearts in which we live together. Though we are different in shape, color and opinion, there is a state wherein we live together. This is the ultimate state that is beyond the distinction of physical shape, social circumstance, or individual opinion. This realm may be depicted as a stream that flows from one person to others, indeed to all beings throughout the world. When this stream is blocked off by the obstacle of one's selfish desires, the water of the stream does not flow into others. In this case, the communication between individuals ceases. We can no longer understand each other correctly, and consequently we develop misunderstandings that cause unpleasant experiences.

According to the teachings of Shakyamuni Buddha, the natural flow of the stream indicates truth, which can penetrate everywhere; the power that stops it is our blind, selfish desire. These blind, selfish desires cause us to suffer spiritually. The teaching of "emptiness" indicates the world of oneness in which we become free from the bondage of self-imprisonment, so we can understand each other naturally and penetrate each other spiritually. In this way, we may attain peace in our hearts. The world of "emptiness" thus expresses the ultimate state of togetherness, unity and peace. Distrust among persons may become a source of increased tension and uneasiness that results in dreadful situations. To trust each other and to work together is the best way to be released from tension and to experience complete ease.

Chapter Five

BUDDHISM IN LIFE

Buddhism for the Modern World

Two travelers were walking through a large field. When they came to the shade of a big tree, they found there the bones and flesh of a great beast. They started a discussion about these remains. One of the travelers had an excellent knowledge of science and art. He wanted to recreate the beast because he knew how to do it and believed that to recreate the original beast was the way to reveal the greatness of human ability. He also thought that it was the only way to use the knowledge he had acquired. The other traveler knew, however, that it was dangerous to reconstruct the beast, for the recreator would be killed by the beast he had reconstructed. This man believed that it was not proper for the first man to use his knowledge in this fashion.

After a long discussion, however, the one who had wanted to use his scientific knowledge won the argument. He began to collect the scattered pieces of the great beast and to reconstruct it. The one who opposed the use of knowledge in this manner and who lost the argument inevitably had to withdraw and run away from the scene. The man of science and art used all the knowledge necessary to recreate the original beast. When he finished his work, however, his life came to an end, for he was killed by the beast he recreated.

The knowledge of natural science and art have occupied a large place in modern civilization. It has greatly contributed to the betterment, welfare, and convenience of human life. One of the strong tendencies that has influenced the mind of modern people is that truth should be proved by the objectively verifiable scientific method. Therefore, anything that cannot be verified through this method is easily denied to have value or existence in truth. In other words, it is easy to find the value of something that is tangible or touchable, but it is difficult to see the value or meaning of that which is intangible or untouchable.

The modern world is sometimes called a materialistic and mechanized civilization. People set great value on matter, technology and capital, but forget the invisible spiritual value of human existence. Consequently, they seem to have become slaves to science and money and to have lost autonomy and human dignity.

We created the atomic bomb through our supreme knowledge of science and technology but we may destroy ourselves with this same creation. We are now in danger. The outcome all depends on our choice; our subjective judgment rather than an objective theory will determine whether or not we survive this crisis.

Money also has a strong position in our minds. Even technology and talent are displaced by money. What is more tragic, though, is that many people readily sell even their own souls for money or material gain and pleasure. In such a world, the morality of honesty is not properly valued. Dishonesty and distrust gradually come to occupy people's minds. As a result, people become isolated from each other. In the course of life, they come to suffer from loneliness and insecurity.

People know the exchange value of things, but forget absolute value. In regard to human life, they know its superficial value but they are ignorant of its inner value. At this point we should turn our eyes from the outer tangible world to our inner selves and reconsider what the real value of human existence is. It is very important to see the realm beyond the objective knowledge of science and technology. In this way humankind can restore its own being. Bearing in mind this aspect of the human being could help modern civilization to contribute more effectively to the well-being of all humans.

The Blessings of Adversity

The great master of classical drama in Europe, William Shakespeare, once said, "Sweet are the uses of adversity." Adversity, which means misfortune or a miserable state of being or suffering, is the kind of situation we would rather not experience or even hear about. However, in human life we will undoubtedly experience such a state of misfortune or adversity.

There are at least two types of reactions to such an unpleasant condition. One is negative, escapism. In this case people do not want to be involved with anything for which they must assume responsibility. Faced by misfortune, they may simply bemoan their condition. Sometimes they may criticize others, or abuse others, because they assume their own misfortune to be someone else's fault. If it really is someone else's fault, they may nag, berate or insult the one at fault. Needless to say, this approach of coping with adverse situations is not right, but rather is the way to death.

The other way is a positive, constructive way of reacting to an undesirable situation. In this case, people attempt to understand the meaning of the adverse experience that they confront and to react positively to improve the situation rather than simply complain. This is the way that Shakyamuni Buddha taught us. In the fundamental teaching of the Four Noble Truths, we learn that we should first recognize the meaning of suffering in life in order that we may understand the reality of human existence. Even though we do not like to think of suffering, the Buddha warned us to investigate and understand it so as to bring enlightenment to our hearts.

Those who have lived in a nice family in which they have had no trouble may complain or grieve when they come across an unexpected adversity. Shakyamuni Buddha emphasized, therefore, that we should learn something meaningful from the experience of misfortune, through which life may become more enriched spiritually; and thus we may attain peace within ourselves. This is what Shakespeare might have meant when he so beautifully said, "Sweet are the uses of adversity."

It was mentioned previously that immediate action to improve a situation or to create better conditions is the most important thing for us to do when we encounter a problem. We should not complain or abuse each other, because while we are doing so, there will be no happy solutions for us, just endless disputes. The positive way of living is expressed in the final teaching of Shakyamuni Buddha, "Both in public and in private, show loving-kindness to others in body, speech and thought; share with others whatever is received as a gift; maintain conduct that supports mindfulness, is praised by the wise, and leads to liberation; and continue in those views that lead to the destruction of suffering and lead to liberation." *(Mahaparinibbana Sutta)*

Self-Reflection

About 150 years ago in Japan, there lived a Zen priest whose name was Ryokan. He loved people and nature, and led a simple life in a humble hermitage. Even now he is still loved by young and old alike.

Once, while staying at a temple in the countryside, he was asked to come and admonish his nephew Umanosuke. Umanosuke was wasting his time in diversions. His family and relatives became so worried about him that they met, talked together, and decided to ask Ryokan to come. Unfortunately, however, Ryokan refused their request, saying "I am not good enough to scold or punish him." A few days later, however, Ryokan developed a desire to see his nephew, so he went back to his native home. His family and relatives were delighted with his visit and expected him to give serious advice to Umanosuke. Uncle Ryokan, however, acted disinterested. He just smiled and did not say a harsh word. After a week, he suddenly said, "I am going back to my temple." The relatives were surprised and complained because he had not said anything to Umanosuke.

When he went to the door and was trying to put on his straw sandals, Umanosuke came and helped him tie the strings. Ryokan looked at him in silence. Unconsciously, his eyes filled with tears of sympathy and compassion. A teardrop fell on the hand of Umanosuke as he was tying the strings of Ryokan's sandals. Looking up with wonder, the boy found his uncle's face full of kindness and love. He suddenly awakened to his uncle's compassion and sympathy toward him, and realized his own past wrongdoing. He sat down on the ground and apologized bowing deeply, "I am sorry uncle ....." When Umanosuke had finished speaking, Ryokan embraced him gently and said, "You are not the only person who has been guilty of such things. The tendency toward diversion is what every person has in their heart. But it is wise that you are now aware of your deeds." Thus Ryokan cried sympathetically with him.

In our own lives, we may easily blame others or criticize their conduct. Yet should we forget so easily to reflect upon ourselves? A teardrop of love from Ryokan led Umanosuke into the profound realm of self-reflection by which he was awakened to true love. If we sincerely appreciate this story, we can find the truth that reproach does not bring about peace, and that only by self-reflection can we gain the promise of real liberation.

Chapter Six

BUDDHISM IN JAPAN

Higan - the Other Shore

Buddhist temples throughout Japan observe what we call the Higan service on the Spring and Autumnal equinoxes. At these times, Japanese Buddhists, young and old, men and women, go to the temple or cemetery to pay respect to their ancestors.

In the *Myogi-shu*, an important Jodo Shu treatise, it says, "A bodhisattva reaches that shore of nirvana, after leaving this shore of life and death, and boards the ship of meditation and crosses the river of illusion." *Higan* literally means "that shore," which is the opposite of *shigan*, or "this shore." "This shore" signifies the world of humanity, of life and death. "That shore" denotes the world of nirvana, of "Buddha". People are living on "this shore," longing for the world of "that shore." We are often suffering in the middle of the "ocean" of illusion, where we can be dissolved by pleasure or can wallow in luxury and vice. We live to pursue self-satisfaction without any consideration for the well-being of others.

Shakyamuni Buddha was born in this world, on this shore. Observing profoundly the sorrow of this world of illusion, he reached that distant shore of nirvana. He showed all humankind the means of crossing the ocean of darkness to the realm of light on that shore, *higan*. These are called the six pathways (Skt. *paramita*, Jp. *haramitsu*) to nirvana.

The first path is generosity *(dana)*. This does not merely mean to give money, but to give support to others in various ways, such as with material goods, helping by physical strength or spiritual inspiration. When we earn a great deal of money or rise to a higher position in society, we are prone to be lax and to fail to maintain proper conduct. This is why the path of right conduct *(sila)* is set forth in the second *paramita*. In the third, the path of endurance *(ksanti)* shows us that we should be patient with each other to live together in humanity. In the fourth, the path of endeavor *(virya)* teaches us that we should not be lazy but should make every effort to attain contentedness. In the fifth, the path of meditation *(dhyana)* suggests that we should not be upset by trivialities and the things of this shore, but should be calm as we consider and try to understand our problems. In the sixth, the path of wisdom *(prajna)* indicates that, since there are often misunderstandings among people and these misunderstandings lead us to hate one another because of false or wrong knowledge, we should endeavor to gain true or right knowledge.

The above interpretation of the six pathways is not an academic one but an attempt to explain the meaning of the teachings in relation to our daily life. The six *paramitas* constitute the universal way for humans to attain ultimate peace, but it is not easy for us to keep them in mind and carry them out, because we are busy living and working everyday. For this reason, we set aside a special day twice a year, in Spring and Fall, so that we may reconsider these teachings, reflect upon ourselves, and pay respect to the innumerable people from the past to the present who have come into our lives and in some way or other influenced it to be better. This is the basic concept of the *higan* observance.

Obon - Remembrance

According to the tradition, one of Shakyamuni Buddha's disciples Maudgalyayana (Mokuren), after enduring practices of profound meditation, attained the ability to see and hear various happenings in the world of the afterlife. When observing the afterlife of his parents with this new vision, he found to his surprise that his mother was suffering from agony in the realm of hungry ghosts (Skt. *preta*, Jp. *gaki*). It puzzled him why his beloved, kindly mother should suffer such misery and pain as this. He rushed to the Buddha, asking how he could help his mother. The Blessed One said that, since his mother had been characterized by selfishness and grasping while she was on earth, she was now reaping the fruits of her greedy conduct. The way she could be liberated depended on Maudgalyayana's piety. The Buddha suggested to him that on July 15, when many monks were going to meet together after a long session of retreat for the rainy season, he should offer them food with reverence and a pure heart. When this offering was made, Maudgalyayana's mother would gain deliverance from the pain of hell.

The Obon service, having its origin in this legend, should receive our special consideration. The acts of Maudgalyayana's mother during this life and the sufferings she experienced in the afterlife can be considered true not only of her but also of all mothers on earth. The love of mothers in raising and protecting their children is great. The efforts of all parents for their children look beautiful, but in fact they may involve some things that cannot be mentioned to others. Parents may be confronted with such situations that inevitably fall in the category of self-centered and unkind acts to others because of their children. Maudgalyayana was aware of the deep love and affection his mother had showered upon him, and made the offering to the monks with a grateful mind.

Thus Obon is the time to have a moment to ourselves to meditate on the affection and efforts our parents have made for us and to pay respect to our forefathers who have given their lives so that we may have a better life. Let us relive with our dear ones the happy days we spent together and find renewed comfort and hope for tomorrow.

Bodhi - Enlightenment

Bodhi Day is the celebration of enlightenment, the day when Siddhartha Gautama became Shakyamuni Buddha. On this day he was enlightened to the truth of himself and the universe, and finally attained real peace and happiness.

It is not hard to look at oneself in a mirror, but what is seen is merely a reflection of oneself. It is difficult, however, to look at one's true self. In order to understand the moon reflecting on the calm surface of the water, we should know first that it is merely a shadow of the real moon shining up in the sky. A story in the legends of the Buddha's previous lives, the *Jatakas*, expresses is clearly:

Once upon a time there were some monkeys that enjoyed looking at the beautiful moon as it was reflected on the bubbles in the water. They tried to catch the moon. One of them jumped into the water, the rest of them waited for a while until he came up. But he did not appear. Then the next one jumped into the water. He did not come back either. Then the rest of the monkeys thought that

there was something wonderful and precious
down in the water. So they jumped into the water
in the same manner, and so not one returned.

The poor monkeys took their own lives, because they mis-
took the beautiful moon on the water for the real moon.
They tried to capture it, but actually it was only a shadow.
A shadow is a shadow, and not reality. When we understand it is a shadow, we do not have to pursue it any
longer. In this way of understanding, the door to truth is
opened for us. In our daily life, however, we often fail to
see our real selves and mistakenly discover the shadow of
ourselves and declare, "I live by myself. This is mine. I
have helped you. I feed the family." Emphasizing "I", each
one of us attaches to our own shadow or our fabricated
self. If someone speaks critically of what I have done, I
might say, "I did it for you, not for myself, so what is
wrong with it? You should just thank me." Man is dis-
posed to think of himself alone and to believe that he can
act and live alone.

Shakyamuni became aware of himself in such a way
that he realized he did not live alone but rather he lived by
the grace of immeasurable blessings from heaven and
earth. When sitting in deep meditation under a *bodhi* tree
(a pippal tree), he had a great experience as he felt the
breath and life of the tree, the air, and the whole universe
surrounding him. At dawn, as the morning star was still
twinkling in the sky, he intuitively "awakened." He discov-

ered himself to be a part of the great life of the world. Thus he was liberated from the world of bondage and selfish individuality and from the illusory world of unreal shadows. He attained the bliss of perfect freedom and realized the truth of the universe. Consequently he became a buddha. This is said to have occurred on December 8th. Therefore, Buddhists throughout the world celebrate this day as Bodhi Day.

APPENDICES

A Chronology of Honen Shonin

A.D.	Japanese Year	Honen's Age	Events
1133	Chojo 2	1	*4th Month* - Born in Mimasaka province (now Okayama Prefecture); named Seishi-maru.
1134	Chojo 3	2	Floods, famine and tuberculosis strike the country.
1141	Ho-en 7	9	*Spring* - Honen's father, Uruma no Tokikuni, killed by Sada-akira. Seishimaru sent to Bodai-ji, his uncle's temple.
			Eisai, the founder of the Zen sect Rinzai-shu, is born.
1145	Ten-yo 2	13	*Spring* - Ascends Mt. Hiei and begins study with Genko.
1146	Kyu-an 2	14	The great fire of Kyoto.
1147	Kyu-an 3	15	Begins study with Koen and is ordained.
1148	Kyu-an 4	16	*Spring* - Begins to study Tendai doctrine.
1150	Kyu-an 6	18	*9th month* - Begins study with Eiku and given the dharma name, Honen-bo Genku.
1156	Hogen 1	24	Visits the Shakado hall on the way to Nara to study and find the way of salvation. Hogen political insurrection.
1159	Heiji 1	27	Heiji political insurrection.
1167	Nin-an 2	35	Taira no Kiyomori becomes chancellor (dajodaijin).
1171	Jo-an 1	39	Kansai becomes Honen's disciple.
1175	Jo-an 5	43	*Spring* - Honen founds his independent Pure Land denomination, Jodo Shu, at Kurodani. Leaves Kurodani for Hirodani. Meets Yurenbo Ensho.
1177	Jisho 1	45	Yurenbo dies. Honen leaves Hirodani for Higashiyama Otani.
1181	Yowa 1	49	Nationwide famine strikes.
1183	Juei 2	51	*7th month* - Minamoto no Yoshinaka invades Kyoto. The only day Honen does not study.

1186	Bunji 2	54	*Autumn* - Ohara Debate (or in 1189).
1190	Kenkyu 1	58	Honen lectures on the *Three Pure Land Sutras (Jodosanbukyo)* at Todai-ji temple in Nara. Shoku becomes Honen's disciple.
1192	Kenkyu 3	60	Kumagai Naozane becomes Honen's disciple. *7th month*- Minamoto no Yoritomo establishes Kamakura military government.
1195	Kenkyu 6	63	Genchi becomes Honen's disciple.
1197	Kenkyu 8	65	Shoko becomes Honen's disciple.
1198	Kenkyu 9	66	Honen writes the *Senchaku Hongan Nembutsu-shu (Passages on the Selection of the Nembutsu in the Original Vow).* Kosai becomes Honen's disciple. Honen attains absorption in the nembutsu *(nembutsu-samadhi).*
1199	Kenkyu 10	67	Shoko is given a copy of the *Senchaku-shu.*
1200	Shoji 2	68	*1st month* - Dogen, founder of the Zen sect Soto-shu, is born. *2nd month* - Honen attends Kansai's deathbed.
1201	Kennin 1	69	Shinran becomes Honen's disciple.
1202	Kennin 2	70	Kanezane ordained by Honen. Chosai becomes Honen's disciple.
1204	Genkyu 1	72	*3rd month* - Ryukan is given a copy of the *Senchaku-shu.* *8th month* - Shoko leaves for Kyushu. *10th month* - The armed monks of Mt. Hiei appeal to Zasu Shinsho to stop the nembutsu. *11th month* - Honen warns the nembutsu followers to conduct themselves properly by issuing the *Seven Article Pledge (Sichikajo Kishomon).*
1205	Genkyu 2	73	Monks from Kofuku-ji temple appeal to the Imperial Court to stop the nembutsu. Shinran is given a copy of the *Senchaku-shu.*
1206	Ken-ei 1	74	Anraku and Juren executed.

1207	Jogen 1	75	*7th month* - Honen leaves Otani for Komatsu-dono. *2nd month* - The nembutsu practice prohibited. *3rd month*- Order for Honen's exile to Tosa issued. Honen leaves Kyoto and, via Muro-no-tsu harbor, arrives on Shikoku island. *4th month* - Kanezane dies. *12th month* - Imperial Order of Honen's pardon issued.
1208	Jogen 2	76	Honen stays at the Kachiodera temple in Osaka.
1211	Kenryaku 1	79	*8th month* - Permitted to return to Kyoto. *11th month* - Honen begins to live at Higashiyama Otani.
1212	Kenryaku 2	80	*23rd day of 1st month* - Honen writes the *One Sheet Document (Ichimai Kishomon)* and gives it to Genchi.*25th of 1st month* - Dies at the age of eighty. Koben (Myo-e) writes the *Zaijarin* to criticize the *Senchaku-shu.*
1220	Jokyu 2		Ji-en writes the *Gukansho,* an account of the Kamakura Era.
1227	Karoku 3		The monks of Mt. Hiei try to exhume Honen's body at the Higashiyama cemetery. Shinku and other disciples of Honen move Honen's body to Nison-in temple. Ryukan, Kua and Kosai exiled.
	Antei 2		*1st month* - Honen's body cremated at Awano.

A Guide to Further Reading

Honen's Major Writings

1. Commentaries on Genshin's *Ojoyoshu* (1145-1175)

2. Commentaries on the *Three Pure Land Sutras (Jodosanbukyo)*

   a) Sanbukyo tai-i [before 1186]

   (Commentary on the General Meaning of the Jodosanbukyo)

   b) Sanbukyo-shaku [circa 1190]

   (Commentaries on the Jodosanbukyo)

3. *Gyakushu seppo (The "Pre-emptive Funeral" Sermons)* [1194]

4. *Senchakushu* [1198]

   (Passages on the Selection of the Nembutsu in the Original Vow)

5. *Ippyaku-shiju-gokajo mondo* [1201]

   (One Hundred Forty-five Questions and Answers)

6. *Shichikajo-kishomon (Seven Article Pledge)* [1204]

7. *Sanmai-hottokuki (Record of Attaining Samadhi)* [1198-1206]

8. *Ichimai-kishomon (The One Sheet Document)* [1212]

9. *Isshi-koshosoku (Reply to a Disciple)* [after 1175]

10. Letters & Personal Writings

In Japanese, these are all found in the *Showa shinshu Honen shonin zenshu*

In English,

-#6, #8, #9 and parts of #5 can be found on

the Jodo Shu Research Institute's English homepage

http://www.jodo.or.jp/jsri/English/Main.html

-#4, the *Senchaku-shu*, Honen's magnum opus, has been published as:

Honen's Senchakushu

translated & edited by the Senchakushu English Translation Project

(Honolulu : The Kuroda Institute, University of Hawaii Press &

Tokyo: Sogo Bukkyo Kenkyujo of Taisho University, May 1998)

The Six Major Biographies of Honen

1. *Chionkoshiki* (1224)

2. *Daigobon Honen Shonin denki* [the *Daigo-bon*] (circa 1242)

3. *Genku Shonin shinikki* [the *Shinikki*] (circa 1237-56)

4. *Honcho Soshi denki ekotoba* [the *Shikan-den*] (1237)

5. *Honen Shonin denki* [the *Kukan-den*] (circa 1312)

6. *Honen Shonin gyojoezu* [the *Shijuhachikan-den*] (circa 1311-1323)

In Japanese, these are all found in the *Honen shonin den zenshu*

In English, #6 has been published as:

Honen the Buddhist Saint : His Life and Teaching

trans. by Harper H. Coates & Ishizuka Ryugaku

(Kyoto: Society for the Publication of Sacred Books of the World, 1949)

also see:

Renegade Monk: Honen and Japanese Pure Land Buddhism

> Soho Machida, trans. Ioannis Mentzas

> (Berkeley: University of California Press, 1999)

English Translations of Major Pure Land Texts

The Three Pure Land Sutras

The Larger *Sukhavativyuha Sutra (Sutra of Immeasurable Life)*

The *Amitayur-dhyana Sutra (Meditation Sutra)*

The Smaller *Sukhavativyuha Sutra (Amida Sutra)*

     in *Sacred Books of the East: Buddhist Mahayana Texts,* vol. 49,

     trans.Max F. Muller & Junjiro Takakusu

     (London: Oxford University Press, 1894)

     Reprint (New York: Dover Publications, 1969).

The Three Pure Land Sutras: A Study and Translation

     Hisao Inagaki

     (Kyoto: Nagata Bunshodo, 1994)

The Land of Bliss - the Paradise of the Buddha of Measureless Light :
Sanskrit and Chinese Versions of the Sukhavativyuha Sutras

     Luis O. Gomez

     (Honolulu: University of Hawaii Press &

     Kyoto: Higashi Honganji Shinshu Otani-ha, 1996)

T'an-luan's Commentary on Vasubandhu's Discourse on the Pure Land
(Ojoron-chu): A Study and Translation

     Hisao Inagaki

     (Kyoto: Nagata Bunshodo, 1998)

Other Books on Pure Land Buddhism

The Pure Land Tradition: History and Development

     eds. James Foard, Michael Solomon, Richard Payne

     (Berkeley, CA: Regents of the University of California &

     Institute of Buddhist Studies, 1996)

The Dawn of Chinese Pure Land Buddhist Doctrine
   Kenneth Tanaka
   (Albany: State University of New York Press, 1990)

River of Fire, River of Water :
An Introduction to the Pure Land Tradition of Shin Buddhism
   Taitetsu Unno
   (New York: Doubleday, May 1998)

Shinran's Gospel of Pure Grace
   Alfred Bloom
   (Tucson: The University of Arizona Press, 1968)

Buddha of Infinite Light
   D.T. Suzuki
   (Boston: Shambhala Publications, 1997)

Jodo Shinshu: Shin Buddhism in Medieval Japan
   James Dobbins
   (Indianapolis: Indiana University Press, 1989)

No Abode: The Record of Ippen
   Dennis Hirota
   (Hawaii: University of Hawaii Press, 1997)

The Teachings Essential for Rebirth: A Study of Genshin's "Ojoyoshu"
   Allan A. Andrews
   (Tokyo: Sophia University Press, 1973)

Books on Japanese Buddhism & Religion

Shapers of Japanese Buddhism
   Koyu Sonoda, Yusen Kashiwahara, eds.
   (Tokyo: Charles E Tuttle Co., 1994)

Foundation of Japanese Buddhism, vols. 1&2
    Daigan & Alicia Matsunaga
    (Los Angeles: Buddhist Books International, 1974)
Zen and Japanese Culture
    D.T. Suzuki
    (Princeton: Princeton University Press, 1970)
Japanese Spirituality
    D.T. Suzuki
    (New York: Greenwood Press, 1988)
Religion and Nothingness
    Keiji Nishitani, trans. Jan Van Bragt
    (Berkeley: University of California Press, 1983)
Ways of Thinking of Eastern Peoples: India, China, Tibet, Japan
    Hajime Nakamura
    (Honolulu: University of Hawaii Press, 1964)
On Understanding Japanese Religion
    Joseph M. Kitagawa
    (Princeton: Princeton University Press, 1987)
Japanese Religion: Unity and Diversity
    Byron Earhart
    (Belmont, CA: Wadsworth Publishing Co., 1970)
Practically Religious: Worldly Benefits
and the Common Religion of Japan
    Ian Reader; George J. Tanabe Jr.
    (Honolulu: University of Hawaii Press, 1998)
Buddhism in Japan: With an Outline of Its Origins in India
    E. Dale Saunders
    (Tokyo: Charles E. Tuttle Co., 3rd printing, 1980)

Update Buddhism in Japan

Kodo Matsunami

(Tochigi, Japan: Kinryuji Searchlight Center, 1993)

Other Books on Mahayana Buddhism

Fundamental Wisdom of the Middle Way :
Nagarjuna's Mulamadhyamakakarika

J. Garfield

(New York: Oxford University Press, 1995)

Emptiness : A Study in Religious Meaning

F. Streng

(New York: Abingdon Press, 1967)

Outlines of Mahayana Buddhism

D.T. Suzuki

(New York: Schocken Books, 1963)

Mahayana Buddhism : the Doctrinal Foundations

Paul Williams

(London: Routledge, 1989)

Dynamic Buddha and Static Buddha

Susumu Yamaguchi

(Tokyo: Risosha, 1958)

Dictionaries

Japanese English Buddhist Dictionary (revised edition)

Shinyu Iwano

(Tokyo: Daito Shuppansha, 1991)

A Dictionary of Japanese Buddhist Terms
Hisao Inagaki
(Kyoto: Nagata Bunshodo, 1984)
A Glossary of Shin Buddhist Terms
Hisao Inagaki
(Kyoto: Nagata Bunshodo, 1995)

Books from Jodo Shu Press

Jodo Shu : A Daily Reference
Edited by the Jodo Shu Research Institute, 1999, 108 pages, US$12
This pocket sized volume offers an official overview of Jodo Shu teachings, practices and history with a detailed three language index of terms.

Amida Buddha and His Pure Land: Three Sutras and One Treatise
Translated by Kenjo S. Urakami, 1997, 258 pages, US$48
The three fundamental sutras for Pure Land Buddhists which Honen compiled for the first time as a single integrated teaching. This translation uses a simplified English helpful to young learners and non-native English speakers.

Words of Dharma
Translated by Dwight Ryokan Nakamura, 1994, 80 pages, US$8
A translation of Chion-in temple's *Go Ho Go*, this is a collection of 62 short anecdotes and messages written by Honen himself. A glossary of terms is also included.

Our St. Honen
Written Ryowa Takahashi & Illust. Rev. Jung Iida, 12 pages, US$4
A short picture book ideal for children tells the story of Honen's early life, ordination as a Buddhist monk, and abandonment of Mt. Hiei to teach the nembutsu to all.

*Price is subject to change when exchange rates vary

How to order the Jodo Shu Publications

When ordering publications, please send US$ cash by registered mail for the book price and shipping charge to "Jodo Shu Press". We will ship the book upon receipt of the fee.

> Jodo Shu Press
> 4-7-4 Shibakoen, Minato-ku,
> Tokyo 105-0011
> Japan

Remark: Surface mail charge is included in the book price. Please add 25% of total price for the air mail. It will take one week by air shipment and about one month by sea shipment.

About the Author

Rev. Sho-on Hattori was born in Aichi Prefecture, Japan, in 1933. He received his B.A. from Taisho University in Tokyo, and his M.A. from the University of Southern California in Los Angeles, U.S.A. He served as a Buddhist minister at the Jodo Shu Betsuin in Los Angeles from 1959 to 1967. He is now a professor emeritus at Tokaigakuen Women's College and the head priest of the Chofuku-ji temple in the city of Tsushima, Aichi Prefecture.

To learn more about Honen and his Pure Land teachings visit the Jodo Shu Research Institute homepage at:
http://www.jodo.or.jp/jsri/English/Main.html